The Architect

Women in Contemporary Architecture

The Architect

Women in Contemporary Architecture

Copyright © The Images Publishing Group Pty Ltd 2001

Published in the United States in 2001 by
Watson-Guptill Publications
a division of BPI Communications, Inc.
770 Broadway, New York, NY 10003
www.watsonguptill.com

Designed by The Graphic Image Studio Pty Ltd
Mulgrave, Australia
Text set in 9-pt Caslon 224

Senior editor: Sylvia Warren, Watson-Guptill Publications

Library of Congress Card Number: 00–110045

ISBN 0-8230-1652-8

First published in Australia in 2001 by
The Images Publishing Group Pty Ltd
6 Bastow Place, Mulgrave, Victoria 3107, Australia
www.imagespublishing.com.au

Printing and binding by Sing Cheong Printing Company Limited,
Hong Kong

First printing, 2001

1 2 3 4 5 6 7/07 06 05 04 03 02 01

Contents

Preface
"Altered Reality"

This book has the urgency of alerting people to the great contributions made by women architects to contemporary architecture, architects whose exceptional vision and design expertise have provided landmark expressions of modern culture. Underlying this celebration of their achievements is the ongoing struggle of these women to achieve professional parity with men in a field long dominated by males. It is dispiriting to repeatedly attend business meetings with only men, as though this represented a true demographic picture of society. Ideally, architecture should embody the rich diversity that globalization has brought to all of our urban environments. An architecture informed by the collective life experience of women, men, people of all ages, and people of all minority groups would be immeasureably enriched.

Some US Demographics

Over the past fifty years, the number of women studying architecture in the United States has steadily increased. Female enrollment in U.S. architecture schools currently averages 35 percent, and in some of the top schools there is actually a 50/50 split of women to men. It is also a fact that the best design work emerging over a ten-year period in those schools has been accomplished equally by women and men. It is inspiring to teach architecture and to be on design juries today, observing firsthand that the most innovative, outstanding work in schools of architecture is being created by women and men in equal numbers.

But What Happens After Graduation?

Exact numbers are hard to come by, but the following estimates are widely accepted. The number of licensed women architects who are principals or partners in firms is about 10 percent overall (most are partners in their own firms); for large firms, the number shrinks to 5 percent. The percentage of licensed women architects in nontraditional jobs is also about 10 percent. The numbers are increasing by small increments every year, but we do not see a commensurate increase in the leadership ranks. In interior design, 81 percent of practitioners are women, yet when major awards are handed out, 50 percent of them go to men. All 21 Pritzker Prize winners are men. Not a single woman has received this prestigious award, considered by many to be the Nobel Prize of Architecture. Itsuko Hasegawa and Zaha Hadid should receive it—to name just two. Another injustice waiting to be rectified concerns the American Institute of Architects (AIA) Gold Medal, given only to men—57 altogether—in all the years of its existence since 1907. By way of contrast, women have received official Nobel Prizes in all the assigned professions, which leaves the architecture profession behind in this regard.

In the United States, only 20 percent of full-time university faculty members in architecture are women and only 10 percent of tenured professors of architecture are women. Female deans constitute less than 4 percent of total administrative leaders. It is significant that in 2000, *Architecture* and *Architectural Record*, two of the most respected architecture magazines in America, carried editorials lamenting the situation and pressing for an end to second-class citizenship for women in the architectural community.

In a male-dominated society, there are a thousand subtle ways of perpetuating bias against women, of pretending to be innocent of discriminatory practices, and of avoiding taking the initiative to bring about change. At this time in history, it is important to show solidarity with struggling women architects, in order to advance their progression to professional equality. When women architects no longer have to remind us that they do not want to be considered one of the best "female architects" but simply one of the best architects, when unqualified recognition is given where recognition is due, then things will be in the right place.

The State of Women in the World

In order to see the obstacles against women in the architectural profession in perspective, we must look at society as a whole. Throughout history, men have dominated all but a tiny number of small societies, meaning that discrimination against women is deep-rooted and difficult to change. In terms of numbers of people, it is the most pervasive form of bias in the world, because it affects half of the world's population.

Although most of the world's governments are committed, on paper, to full equality for women, the reality is otherwise. Certain observations should be highlighted:[1]

- Religious fundamentalism is on the rise, which will lead to heightened legal and social restrictions on women.
- Sometimes, keeping women "in their place" is a literal undertaking.
- In almost every society and culture, boys are preferred and privileged over girls.
- Worldwide (excluding agriculture) women earn an average of 75 percent of men's pay.
- Around the world, women are far more likely than men to hold low-paying jobs. (In the UK, the number of women in low-wage jobs is 31 percent, compared with 13 percent of men; in the US, the figures are 33 percent for women, 20 percent for men.)
- Much of women's work—agricultural, childcare, caring for the elderly, housework—is unpaid.
- The "glass ceiling" that keeps women out of the top, higher-paid, prestige jobs may be cracked in spots, but it is still there. The United Nations estimates that women will have to wait until the year 2490 to achieve equal representation with men in the higher echelons of economic power.
- In many countries, there is a further discrimination: age. Younger women are strongly preferred as employees to the extent that older women are nowhere to be seen. Women of age become invisible.
- In the United Nations General Assembly, 20 percent of the delegates are women.
- In most countries, men gained the right to vote before women. Almost everywhere, votes for women have been strongly resisted.

- In no government in the world is the percentage of women who are elected representatives proportionate to their number in the population. On average, it is: 40 percent in Sweden, Norway, Denmark, Finland, and Germany; 20 percent in Canada, Spain, Italy, and China; 10 percent in the US, South America, France, Eastern Europe, the UK, Ireland, Russia, and Australia. Many of the remaining countries in the world have less than 5 percent or no women who are elected representatives.

The Forces for Change

In the face of societal norms that hinder women's status and professional mobility, certain key philosophers and writers have helped to foster a new way of thinking. After the practical gains achieved by the courageous movement of the suffragists, Simone de Beauvoir's 1949 book *The Second Sex* broke entirely new philosophical ground and provided a powerful beacon for women and feminist organizations all over the world. According to de Beauvoir, under male-dominated social systems, women are "the Other"; throughout history, women have been conditioned from birth to believe that men are superior to women. She said, "One is not born, but rather becomes, a woman."

Jean-Paul Sartre, de Beauvoir, and Albert Camus, as existentialists, developed a far-reaching and profound nonreligious philosophy that holds that one's fate is in one's own hands. Religions traditionally do not provide a vehicle for women to emerge as equals in society. Most of the largest organized religions have institutionalized policies of male dominance, and most place an authority above the individual. Placing maximum trust in an individual's own capabilities, rather than some preordained "nature," gives women and men equal dignity. In judging the impact of one's actions, it is useful to think in terms of the individual choosing for all people: "What if everybody repeated my choice?" In turn, the potential for change can be seen as a serious responsibility for all individuals. If men and women were themselves to place equal value on their thoughts, skills, and roles, and to take equal responsibility for taking action to promote change in society, it could mean the end of discrimination.

Other writers and editors have addressed vital issues in society that influence the status of women. The work of deconstructionists like Jacques Derrida, who question the validity of all laws passed in societies dominated by white males, is seen as a call to action by many female professionals. Derrida states, "In our institutions and in our work, while keeping the memory of the past, we must inaugurate something absolutely new." Leading feminist author Helen Cixous says: "For women to speak strongly in public is something often seen as rash, a transgression. A double anguish, for even if she transgresses, her words almost always fall on deaf masculine ears, which can only hear language that speaks in the masculine."

Over the last few decades, a number of feminist anthologies have been published of writings by women from developing countries, such as Saskia Wieringa's book *Subversive Women*, which clearly show how women have always subverted codes designed to proscribe the spaces in which they should move, extending the boundaries of social space and empowering themselves, as well as actively resisting prevailing regressive authorities. These writings are evidence that a basic cultural exchange among women from completely different backgrounds is possible, wherever women have the means to extend their intellect and skills beyond a survival-based focus. At the same time, it must be acknowledged that there are some women whose words and actions are undermining the movement toward equality. *No Middle Ground: Women and Radical Protest*, a collection of essays about activist women on both the right and the left (Kathleen Blee, ed.) demonstrates that activism can transform and challenge the status quo, but can also be used to reinforce established gender hierarchies.

Failure Is Impossible

Susan B. Anthony, the great suffragist and abolitionist, stands for many as the ultimate fighter for equality and liberty for women. "Failure is impossible" were her final public words. The following lines from William Butler Yeats, originally meant for Irish freedom fighters, were also true of Susan B. Anthony, and of all women and men who have struggled for human rights and full equality:

They shall be remembered forever

They shall be alive forever

They shall be speaking forever

The people shall hear them forever.

Moving Toward Equality

The beautiful and essential differences between women and men should be respected and celebrated, and at the same time their contributions to society valued equally. Women and men, as individuals and designers, are equals and must be regarded as such in every important aspect of what it means to be human. Such human attributes as intellect, character, courage, leadership, imagination, and creativity are not related to gender in any way. Architects—and indeed all creative artists, who are by nature innovators in society—have a responsibility to point the way for other professions. The contemporary philosopher Jean-Francois Lyotard writes: "The innovation of the work of art and architecture take on a political significance as acts that disturb an established status quo and force us to think again; the political is revolutionized by the avant-garde."

Historically, creative artists, and institutions devoted to the fine arts, have not always led the way to a more open-minded approach to women and the issue of equality. In the seventeenth and eighteenth centuries, women artists who achieved success often did so primarily by treating subjects of relevance to women, such as motherhood. In the nineteenth century, women artists like Mary Cassatt in the United States and Marie Bashkirtseff in France were instrumental in paving the way for women to be admitted to exhibiting societies and art schools, but for much of the twentieth century, the record was dismal.

1   Sources: Joni Seager, *The State of Women in the World*; AFL-CIO Fact Sheet (www.aflcio.org/womenf_around.htm).

Today, the situation is very different. Museums all over the world are reconfiguring their collections to display more works by women artists. Art critics, literary critics, and feminist historians and philosophers are calling for far-reaching revisions of the canons to include the contributions of women to art and architecture, literature, music, and philosophy.[2] Today, it is a most exhilarating experience to see contemporary master artists Jenny Holzer's and Richard Serra's dialogues with Frank Gehry's Bilbao Guggenheim museum, dialogues that are triumphs in recognition of the contribution of both men and women to art and architecture. (Holzer is no stranger to progressive creativity; over two decades ago in New York City's Times Square her groundbreaking work *Truisms* appeared, consisting of mammoth LED messages—*Abuse of Power Comes As No Surprise, Everyone's Work Is Equally Important, Most People Are Not Fit to Rule Themselves*, and others—which remain a lasting contribution to the body of socially conscious art.)

Apart from the leading women architects presented in this book, there are many women with flourishing careers within the field of architecture: critics, writers, researchers, teachers, and curators who are making significant contributions. Among them should be mentioned Joan Oakman, Peggy Deamer, Ada Louise Huxtable, Mildred Friedman, Phyllis Lambert, Diane Lewis, Andrea Kahn, Beatrice Colomina, Amanda Reeser, Rosemarie Bletter, Ashley Schafer, Silvia Kolbowski, Jennifer Bloomer, Victoria Newhouse, Cynthia Davidson, Nina Libeskind, Rysia Suchecka, Jill Lerner, Danielle Smoller, Mabel Wilson, and many others. Providing remarkable innovation, architects/artists Elizabeth Diller, Maya Lin, and Iole Alessandrini are merging art and architecture in the most meaningful and seamless ways.

The Future for Women Architects Is the Future of Architecture

In order to eventually realize the possibilities for women architects worldwide, it is important to make an assessment of what kinds of changes can realistically be made now. Large human rights and women's organizations will of course play a crucial role, but actions taken by smaller groups and by individuals are equally important. Changes that bring equality for women must be made, and very soon, before more time and opportunities are lost. Awards could and should be given to two or three designers/architects at once, including distinguished female and male architecture teams, such as Elizabeth Diller and Ricardo Scofidio; Billie Tsien and Todd Williams; Jin Ah Park and Jonathan Ward; Mac Scogin, Merrill Elam, and Lloyd Bray; Laurie Hawkinson and Henry Smith-Miller; and so on. Architecture is a team effort.

There are other basic steps that must be taken. Architecture firms have a responsibility to make it much easier for women to be both mothers and professionals. Additionally, there are too many architecture firms today that have few, if any, women among their design and management leaders. When women become principals, partners, or design leaders, it is important not to be guilty of tokenism. There are plenty of talented, accomplished, and innovative women architects, many of whom are brilliant managers. Those are the people who should be promoted.

Looking optimistically to the future, we can place an exciting dual trust in the parallel revolutions that are occurring in our times, where more women are taking strong creative leadership roles in architecture and at the same time avant-garde design is expanding to new horizons. When they succeed and unite, the impact is awesome. We are transformed both individually and globally into a totally new, magnificent reality.

—Peter Pran, AIA, MNAL
Seattle, 2000

---

2   See, for example, Whitney Chadwick's *Women, Art & Society*; Frances Borzello's *A World of Our Own: Women As Artists Since the Renaissance*; and *The Feminist Reader* (Catherine Belsey and Jane Moore, eds.).

Introduction

The gender issues surrounding architecture are extraordinarily complex and, frequently, highly emotionally charged. Even the title of this book generated controversy: The original title, *The Female Architect,* was rejected because it highlighted the fact that the architects whose work is featured here are women, when most want to be considered just as architects. All want their work to be read on its own merits.

Architecture grows and develops according to the challenges it faces. Taking up the challenge of refuting the gender divide and welcoming intelligent input, from whatever source, will benefit a profession that, by definition, is serving the people for whom it works and therefore needs to operate within a collaborative framework, one offering equal opportunities according to talent rather than gender. In the second year of the new millennium, such is not the case.

Statistics from the UK indicate that in the years 1909 and 1989, the percentage of architects in Britain who were women was the same—a shocking 9 percent! Since 1996, there has been a fractional improvement (estimates range from 10 to 11 percent), but the number is still appallingly low, especially when compared with the percentage of women doctors (50 percent) and solicitors (30 percent). If the number of women architects continues to grow at the present rate, their representation in the profession might just achieve parity by the year 3000.

Another dismal fact is that the number of women entering schools of architecture is inversely related to the number of women who go on to practice architecture. Across the UK, on average, 32 percent of the students entering architecture schools are women; in London, the figure is closer to 50 percent. How do we reconcile these numbers with the low number of women who are practicing in the field? The issue is an international one. In the United States, from 40 to 50 percent of students working toward their master's degree in architecture are female, but only 10 percent of licensed architects in firms are women.

Although the statistics are far from encouraging, efforts are being made to assess the situation and determine what might be done about it. In the UK, construction industry contractors are required to put 5 percent of their profits toward further research into the progress of the industry. The Construction Industry Training Board, which is mandated to ensure that some of these monies go into research that will benefit the future of the industry, has established the Construction Industry Best Practice Programme, which investigates methods for improving working conditions within the industry. Under the previously stated assumption that breaking down gender distinctions will benefit the industry as a whole, it is to be hoped that programs addressing these issues will be developed. However, many observers, including architect Sally Kirk Walker, who works in York, England, feel that neither the construction industry nor established architectural organizations are doing enough. She notes that WISE (Women into Science and Engineering) buses have been visiting UK schools for almost twenty years, encouraging girls to follow career paths in science and engineeering, yet the Royal Institute of British Architects (RIBA) has not spearheaded a similar drive, nor have any of the nationally based construction groups.

Individually, of course, RIBA members have taken action. Annette Fischer, who has been a president of the RIBA Council in London as well as running her own practices, has championed the cause of both women and minority architects. She has made a significant contribution toward smashing the "glass ceiling" frequently hanging over these groups. Fischer believes that the more people like herself become involved in mainstream architecture, the less likely people will be to accept the stereotype of the successful architect as a white male superstar. The more we see the female architect as a powerful influence, the more young women will be encouraged to join the profession and will be able to stay there despite the pressures. At the same time, the fact that more and more developer clients are nonwhite females will foster broad-based input from community groups of all types.

It is illuminating (albeit a bit unsettling) to look at cinema's treatment of architects. For decades, the prototypical architect was *The Fountainhead's* Howard Roark, portrayed on film by Gary Cooper in 1949. Roark, very loosely modeled after Frank Lloyd Wright, was a powerful, brilliant male, an architect who dynamited his work rather than see his ideas compromised. Paul Newman's character in *The Towering Inferno* and Richard Gere's in *Intersection* are cut out of the same cloth, and Woody Harrelson's architect in *Indecent Proposal* is given to quoting one of this century's male architectural icons, Louis Kahn. There are some exceptions to the cinematic rule that architects are powerful, passionate, obsessive, arrogant—and ultimately successful—white males, including Wesley Snipes in *Jungle Fever*, Brian Dennehy in *The Belly of an Architect*, Kimberly Williams in *Father of the Bride II*, and Michelle Pfeiffer in *One Fine Day*. But Williams and Pfeiffer, and Sharon Stone, Richard Gere's luxury-loving architect-wife in *Intersection*, are hardly role *models* for women considering architecture as a profession.

Away from the movies, in the real world, women are just as likely as men to have the five key skills that today's architect needs:

- The ability to listen to and understand the needs of the client.
- The ability to work with a large number of people, with different skills, at any given time.
- The ability to present an authoritative and confident approach.
- The ability to negotiate with planners, site workers, and so on.
- Design competence.

What of the idea that women are not as good as men at projecting an image of power à la Howard Roark? Perhaps women in general are not quite so likely as men to play the hero, but this is not because women lack the qualities that would make them superb superstars, but rather that this model often does not fit with the ways in which women operate.

In a recent lecture, Itsuko Hasegawa spoke of the intense collaborative efforts that are made in the development of her buildings, dwelling on many aspects that may not be given the same emphasis by her male counterparts. Still, it is undeniable that almost all of today's high-profile architects are men, which perhaps has much to do with how men like to present themselves and their work. In the field of architecture, the strong, confident, and even arrogant personality and method of presentation tend to hit the headlines, as well as satisfy clients' desires.

Another stereotypical notion that has to be faced concerns what women—and men—are best qualified to design. When I first started working as an architect, I was asked to design the kitchens of houses specifically because my boss felt that I, as a woman, would be best placed to do this. Although I was perfectly capable of discussing with the future owners what they would like from their kitchens and designing what they wanted, any man could have done the same.

Still another stereotype that should be eradicated is the idea that women create soft, curvy, intuitive, "subjective" architecture. Would anyone dare to say that Frank Gehry's wonderfully curvaceous buildings are the result of a woman's influence? Although our associations might lead us to categorize one building as masculine, and another as feminine, there is nothing *intrinsically* "masculine" or "feminine" about good architecture. That is not to say that a female architect might not want to use the signature style of a male architect, or vice versa. For example, Philip Johnson, one of the most influential architects of this century, designed the gatehouse for his Glass House estate in New Canaan in the style of Zaha Hadid.

Many women architects who are partners in firms in which the other partner is male deplore that fact they do not always get equal recognition. A television program in the United States credited the design of the Sainsbury Wing of the National Gallery in London to: "Robert Venturi and Denise Scott Brown: A partnership in architecture." However, Denise Scott Brown was understandably appalled when the program was broadcast by the BBC as "Robert Venturi: Back to the future." In a 1989 book, *Architecture: A Place for Women* (edited by Ellen Perry Berkely), Scott Brown and a wide variety of other architects tell a selection of horror stories about the discrimination they have suffered in their fight to practice as architects.

Many practicing women architects in the past were able to succeed only because they chose a career instead of marriage, while their male counterparts managed to have both. (How often do you hear a *man* asked how he manages to juggle a career with marriage and children?) Over the years, the career vs. family dilemma has probably been the factor most responsible for keeping more women from becoming full-time practicing architects. One solution to this problem is the husband–wife partnership where the partners share parental responsibilities, such as school runs and trips to the doctor. Such arrangements are positive advances, not only for the woman architect, but also for the family unit.

It is important to recognize that women architects do not speak with one united voice about how they perceive themselves within the profession. Although many do say that the contributions of women are not sufficiently recognized within the "superstar" structure that reflects success in the architectural world, others feel that the problems faced by women in the profession are not as great as those faced by other minorities, and that the advantages outweigh the disadvantages. Is is also important to understand that there is more parity today between female and male architects than in past decades, a progression made possible, in large part, by the work of women who made major contributions to the field:

• Louise Blanchard Bethune (1856–1913) was the first woman to be accepted into the American Institute of Architects, in 1888, and the first woman to be made a fellow, in 1889. In 1892–93 she was invited to submit a design for the World's Columbian Exposition in Chicago, but declined on the grounds that she had not been offered a fair honorarium. Bethune had a strong dislike for single-residence architecture. She rejected the pigeonholing of women into house design, which she knew from her own experience to be the worst-paid and most frustrating job for any architect. A music store in Buffalo, New York designed by Bethune was one of the first buildings in the country with a steel frame and poured concrete slabs. The Renaissance-style Layfayette Hotel in Buffalo, designed by Bethune in 1904, still stands.

• Julia Morgan (1872–1957) was the only woman to graduate from the University of California—Berkeley College of Engineering in 1894 and the first women to pass the entrance examination at the famous Ecole des Beaux-Arts in Paris. During her career she designed hundreds of buildings: houses, conference centers, houses of worship, clubs, schools, hospitals, and gymnasiums. Many of her buildings, including William Randolph Hearst's castle at San Simeon, Bow Bay House at Lake Tahoe, Nevada, and the Livermore House in San Francisco, are famous. Although she is often included in lists of architects who were part of the Arts and Crafts movement in the United States, her work resists classification. Julia Morgan commands respect and interest—both as a pioneering female in the field and as a brilliant architect.

• Although Eileen Gray (1879–1976) is better known—at least to nonarchitects—for her furniture designs (in 1922 she opened Galerie Jean Desert in Paris to sell her own furniture and lacquerware), her architectural theories and designs have been influential. Gray's architectural projects were exhibited in Le Corbusier's pavilion at the 1937 Paris Exposition, and a visit to one of her masterpieces, E.1027, at Roquebrune in the south of France, is a must for anyone interested in the history of modern architecture. She absorbed modernist theory, but was critical of certain doctrinaire aspects of modernism. As she put it, "A house is not a machine to live in. It is the shell of man, his extension, his release, his spiritual radiance."

• Charles Eames and Ray Kaiser (1907–78) met at the Cranbrook Academy of Art in Bloomfield, Michigan, in the late 1930s, beginning a remarkable creative collaboration. They married in 1941, then moved to California and set up their own design and architectural practice. Like Eileen Gray, Charles and Ray Eames are better known for their furniture than for their buildings; many of their classic designs have been selling steadily since they were introduced in the 1940s and '50s. Yet the Eames' contribution to architecture was significant, for they were articulate advocates of high-quality affordable housing, mass-production techniques, and new materials and construction technologies. Although Charles Eames is listed as the architect of the couple's own house, in Pacific Palisades, California, in reality the building—a unique blend of factory-produced components and innovative modernist design—was the result of a collaborative process.

• Another husband-wife team who made important contributions to the body of twentieth-century architecture were Alison Smithson (1928–93) and Peter Smithson, who worked together for almost fifty years. The Smithsons, strong proponents of an architectural style that came to be called "The New Brutalism," consciously and deliberately opposed the canon of the "white modern" (their own term), and the then-prevailing fixation on functionalism. Opposing what they saw as the deplorable state of urban architecture in England, Alison and Peter Smithson were among the few architects prepared to make something serious of the brutalist style. Two of their buildings, the Economist Building in London and their school at Hunstanton in Norfolk, both exquisitely planned and finely detailed, hold up today, a half century later, as thoroughly modern buildings.

It is too early to say which of the thirty-three architects featured in this book will be accorded the same respect by architectural historians as the women listed above. And, of course, there are many more contemporary women architects whose work deserves attention and could have been included. Yet I think that this particular grouping is representative of the wide range of architectural styles, and the range of intellectual and social concerns, to be found among today's practicing women architects.

Irena Bauman, an activist who works to promote the role of women in design and construction, is a strong believer in collaboration, and her firm often includes artists on their design teams. Bauman's practice, Leeds-based Bauman Lyons, is committed to an architecture that works within an overall strategic urban and social context.

Ann Beha, who heads her own firm in Boston, believes that relevance, rather than a particular style, is the key to good architecture. The unique identity of each project emerges from a shared vision of architect and client and, in the case of public projects, the people who will use the building.

Caroline Bos and her husband Ben Van Berkel are interested in the theoretical underpinnings of architectural practice, the global context in which urban architects work. UN Studio, which they co-founded in 1998, comprises a network of specialists in architecture, urban design, and infrastructure.

Since leaving Ron Arad Associates to start her own firm, **Alison Brooks** has designed an astonishing range of project types, from street furniture to an entire hotel complex. The March 2000 issue of *Architectural Review* said of Brooks: "The revolution in hotel design began with Ian Schrager and Phillipe Starck and, later, Jean Nouvel. Brooks takes it a step further."

Although Benoît Cornette, **Odile Decq**'s partner in life as well as in their practice, was killed in a tragic automobile accident over two years ago, Decq still adheres to the principles the two of them developed over the years. She has a keen grasp of architectural theory, and, at the same time, an uncompromising commitment to creative innovation.

In 1999, New York's **Elizabeth Diller**–Ricardo Scofidio partnership was awarded a John D. and Catherine T. MacArthur Foundation Fellowship, grants awarded annually to Americans who "will likely, sooner or later, make a significant difference in human thought and action." The firm plans to use the money to pursue a long-held goal of creating "an alternative form of architectural practice that unites design, performance, and electronic media with cultural and architectural theory and criticism."

Julie Eizenberg works with her partner, Hank Koning, from their office in Los Angeles. Together they have designed numerous award-winning buildings, from high-end *Architectural Record* houses to affordable housing that is both user-friendly and environmentally sound. She supports "green" architecture, and her approach is both innovative and commonsensical.

In addition to being an outstanding architect and influential teacher, **Merrill Elam**, of Mack Scogin Merrill Elam Architects, based in Atlanta, Georgia, is an active member of a number of architectural organizations at both the state and national levels. In both practice and theory, she emphasizes the need to continually re-examine architecture's place within the greater social fabric.

Karen Fairbanks received the first of many awards for excellence in architecture when she was a graduate student at the Columbia University School of Architecture in New York. Marble • Fairbanks, the firm she co-partners with Scott Marble in New York, is known both for its innovative and highly detailed loft designs and for the importance it attaches to the theoretical dynamic between a given design and the total context in which that design will exist.

If a cross-section of nonarchitects, architects, and students were asked to name the single most influential woman in architecture today, a large percentage of them would probably say, **Zaha Hadid**. Hadid's 1989 Vitra Fire Station in Weil am Rhein, Germany, is almost universally acknowledged as a masterpiece. Recent high-profile projects such as the Millennium Dome's Mind Zone and the Contemporary Arts Center in Cincinnati have attracted international attention, and Hadid's famously outspoken voice can be heard, as a keynote speaker and/or panel member, at architectural forums all over the world.

Frances Halsband, whose distinguished career in architecture spans four decades, practices in New York City, with R.M. Kliment & Frances Halsband Architects. Like most of the architects in this book, Halsband's contributions to the world of architecture go far beyond her built work. She is an active teacher and lecturer, sits on various advisory boards, and publishes an important quarterly journal on sustainable design, the Design History Foundation's *Places*.

Sisters **Gisue Hariri** and **Mojgan Hariri** are at once architects, philosophers, and visionaries, and since they co-founded Hariri & Hariri in 1986, their work—both the real and the virtually real—has received wide exposure. A 1998 design for a Connecticut home is on the cover of *New American House 3* (Watson-Guptill, January 2000).

Jane Harrison's academic background includes music, mathematics, and computer science, and her approach to architectural theory incorporates her knowledge of all three disciplines. Atopos, the London– and New York–based firm in which Harrison and her husband, David Turnbull, are co-partners, has been widely exhibited. The exhibition titles—e.g., *In the Midst of Things*; *Unquiet Urbanism*; *Intimate Space*; *City, Space + Globalization*; *Unmapping the Earth: Space/Fire*—are a clue to the depth of their intellectual concerns.

The compelling image on the cover of this book, a shimmering triple-layer perforated screen trellis that encloses the rooftop garden and patio area of a private residence in Tokyo yet looks as though it belongs in an enchanted forest, is by **Itsuko Hasegawa**. Hasegawa, one of Japan's most widely respected architects, likens making architecture to the act of creating a poem or a musical composition.

Keeping abreast of theory, which involves ongoing investigation into the changing role of architecture in today's society, is key to all of **Laurie Hawkinson**'s practice. Called "ever-insurgent" in a recent issue of *Architecture* magazine (in that journal, most definitely a compliment), Hawkinson and her partner, Henry Smith-Miller, work in harmony with many insurgent talents from related fields.

Christine Hawley has long been an inspiring example, both as architect—first as partner in the world-renowned firm Cook and Hawley and more recently as principal of her own practice—and as educator. Hawley, who has been dean of the Faculty of the Built Environment at London's prestigious Bartlett School since 1999, regards an appreciation of situations and conditions that improve living and working environments as a crucial component of her architectural commitment.

Margaret Helfand's early career in architecture included work with Archigram, a London-based group of architects and designers whose ever-changing brand of modernism incorporated each new advance in materials and structural technology. In 1981 she started her own practice in New York, and in 1999 became one of three principals in Helfand Myerberg Guggenheimer, a firm committed to meticulous attention to what she calls the "three axes" of architecture: geometry, structure, and materials.

Katharine Heron believes that in the UK, class prejudice, even more than gender bias, has led to a lack of diversity in architecture. She also believes that it is crucial for architects to get the relationship with the client right. Chair of the Department of Architecture at the University of Westminster and co-principal of London's Feary + Heron Architects, Heron has ample opportunity to disseminate those beliefs.

For a quarter century, **Patty Hopkins** has worked with her husband, Michael, in London's Michael Hopkins and Partners. Though the firm bears his name, Patty Hopkins has been a key principal since the outset. Her contributions enrich every facet of the partnership, whose work has earned most of the major awards given in the field.

The work of **Cathi House**, of the San Francisco-based firm House + House, reflects a wide variety of multicultural influences absorbed through years of extensive travel. House is a person of seemingly limitless creative talent, and her involvement in such crafts as weaving, spinning, painting, rug making, and cabinetmaking imbue her work, and indeed all of the work of House + House, with a unique warmth and intimacy, on a genuinely human scale.

Eva Jiricna's dual training as an architect and engineer in Czechoslovakia, and her understanding of what materials can and cannot do, allows her to design both exteriors and important interior architectural details, notably the marvelous glass and steel staircases she has created for retail shops. Jiricna, who teaches architecture in Prague and is sought after as a lecturer and symposium leader, has been an outspoken critic of the way her design for the Millennium Dome's Faith Zone was compromised.

Sulan Kolatan's work comes by its international flavor naturally, as she was educated in Turkey, Germany, and the United States, and maintains a strong presence in all three countries. New York's Kolatan/MacDonald Studio is known for experimentally extreme designs—exterior and interior, built and unbuilt—and their work is in the permanent collections of several major museums.

Eve Laron began her career in Australia at a time when bias against women in certain professions, including architecture, was widespread. In the early 1970s, she was made partner in a firm she had been practicing with for almost a decade, prompting two male associates to resign rather than work for a female boss. Today, she heads her own firm, and is an activist on two fronts, fighting for environmentally sound design and for the increased presence of women in architecture and related fields.

MJ Long, senior partner in one London practice (Long & Kentish, with Rolfe Kentish) and sole owner of another, has studied and worked with some outstanding creative talent during the course of her long and distinguished career, including Paul Rudolph, Vincent Scully, James Stirling, Charles Gwathmey, Richard Serra, and Nancy Graves. Long and Kentish worked with Colin St. James Wilson over a period of thirty years on the British Library, so of course library design is both a passion and a source of commissions, but Long's firms are also known for museum and gallery design, restoration and preservation, and artists' studios.

Carme Pinós and Enric Miralles, who were partners from 1983 until 1991, designed numerous buildings that attracted international attention. Since splitting with Miralles to start her own practice, Pinós has established her own reputation for design excellence, and Estudio Carme Pinós has been awarded commissions to do an astonishing variety of projects, from a pedestrian footbridge (Alicante) to a hotel (Palma de Mallorca).

The offices of **Regina Pizzinini** and her partner, Leon Luxemburg, span two continents—North America (Los Angeles) and Europe (Luxembourg)—and their designs reflect both a distinctly European style and an American zest for living. It was Charles Moore who convinced them to come to the United States, and his influence is evident in their exuberant and playful use of primary colors and strong geometric shapes.

Kazuyo Sejima practices under the auspices of two firms: her own, and Kazuyo Sejima + Ryue Nishizawa & Associates. Projects completed over the last fifteen years range from minimalist one-off residences to cultural centers and large apartment complexes. Sejima is known not only as a superb architect, but as a master of interior details, such as architectural surface materials, lighting, and even furniture.

In 1977, **Laurinda Spear** became a founding principal of Arquitectonica (ARQ), a Miami-based firm with an international reputation for designing projects that combine memorable imagery with unique regional identity. An artist, marathon runner, mother of six, and highly respected designer of tiles, fabrics, and architectural glass, Spear co-leads ARQ (with husband Bernardo Fort-Brescia) with spirit and determination.

Billie Tsien has worked with her husband Tod Williams since 1977, and they have been partners for over twenty years. Both believe that the worlds of architecture and fine arts are inextricably connected, and the extraordinary range of projects that Tod Williams Billie Tsien and Associates have produced—from light, set, and costume design to award-winning houses and lofts to master planning for world-class museums—attests to the strength of that belief.

Nanako Umemoto and Jesse Reiser are another hugely successful husband-wife team. Working from their studio in the heart of New York City, they collaborate on projects ranging from houses to large-scale urban developments, from furniture design to landscape architecture. Whatever the scale, Reiser + Umemoto never design according to rigid, traditional patterns, relying instead on a visionary analysis of the complex relationships among structure, site, and the larger urban context.

An architect, teacher, and activist committed to promoting diversity in the field, **Sarah Wigglesworth** has become increasingly visible in the architectural community. She believes strongly that architects should continually explore new approaches to financing, to the collaborative process, and to creative uses of technology. The goal should be to develop designs that are at once sustainable, affordable, and beautiful.

I believe that the life and work of every one of these women is of pivotal importance, both because of the intrinsic merit of the work and because the women themselves are wonderful role models.

—Maggie Toy
London, 2000

A note on the Design Statements: Initially, all the architects were asked to make a "statement of most challenging project design"—either a description of a particularly challenging project or the architect's perspective on the challenge of architecture. Although there was tremendous variation in how the architects chose to respond, we decided not to impose an artificial consistency. Many of the Design Statements *are* about the "most challenging" project; many are not. At least one is but a sentence in length. In all cases, we have let the architects speak for themselves.

Bibliography

Hasegawa, I. *Itsuko Hasegawa*. Architectural Monograph, no. 31. London: Academy Editions, 1993.

Lorenz, C. *Women in Architecture: A Contemporary Perspective*. London: Trefoil Publications Ltd., 1990.

Wollstonecraft, M. *A Vindication of the Rights of Women*. First published 1792; first in Everyman's Library, 1929.

Agrest, D., Conway, P. & Kanes Weisman, L. *The Sex of Architecture*. New York: Harry N. Abrams, 1996.

Betsky, A. *Building Sex*. New York: William Morrow, 1995.

SD 90-06 Women in Architecture. Tokyo: Kajima Institute Publishing, 1990.

FX, Sex & Gender (December/January 1996–97). London: ETP Ltd., 1996.

McQuiston, L. *Suffragettes to She Devils*. London: Phaidon, 1997.

Riera Ojeda, O. *Hariri & Hariri*. New York: The Monacelli Press, 1995.

Melhuish, C. *Odile Decq & Benoît Cornette*. London: Phaidon, 1996.

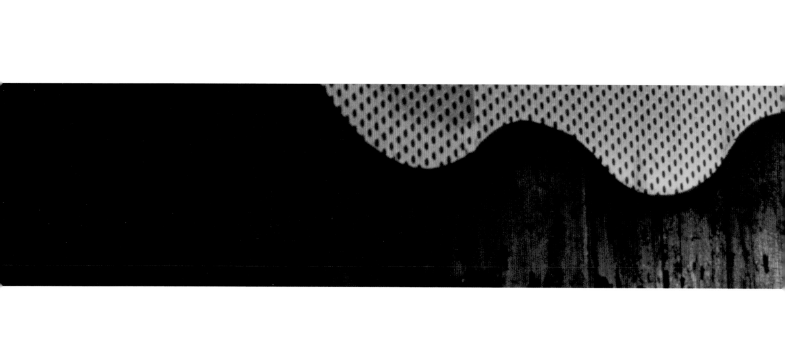

The
Architect

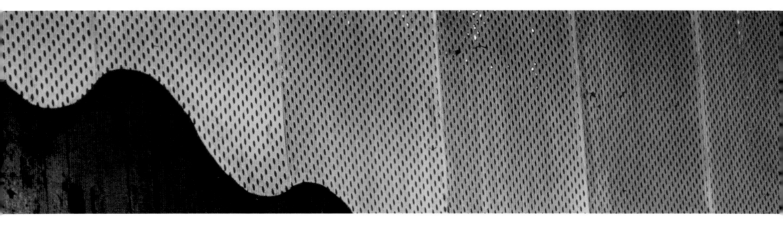

Irena Bauman
United Kingdom

"As architects, we are forever 'bridging gaps'—between theory and practice, inside and outside, art and science; between drawing and constructing, and often between a client's requirements and our own visions. The most successful architecture can only happen when there is no gap to bridge between the client's and her architect's aspirations."

PROFESSIONAL HISTORY

Irena Bauman graduated from Liverpool University School of Architecture in 1981. Since 1992, she has been a partner in Bauman Lyons Architects, a Leeds firm with a wide range of clients and project types. She is a qualified project manager and a frequent lecturer around the country.

Bauman is a founding member of Women in Design and Construction, a pressure group whose purpose is to promote the role of women in design and construction. She is also a member of Leeds Architecture and Design Initiative, and of the Architecture Sub-Group, which advises the Leeds City Council on major urban design and planning issues. Recently, Bauman has been invited to sit on the Art Council of England Architecture & Build Environment Advisory Group, and on the Design Review Committee of the Commission for Architecture & Built Environment—both national committees concerned with promoting good design and innovation in architecture.

Selected Awards

Royal Institute of British Architects (RIBA) Architecture Award, for Bridlington Promenade, 2000

Commendation in National Civic Trust Awards, for Bridlington Promenade, 1999

Leeds Architecture Award, for office conversion of no. 31, The Calls, Leeds, 1999

Leeds Architecture Award, for Holdforth Court (Commendation), 1996

Pub Design of the Year, for Dry Dock, 1995

Leeds Architecture Award, for Sheltered Housing at Whincup Gardens (individual award), 1990

Selected Publications

Melvin, Jeremy. *Young British Architects*. Basel, Switzerland: Birkhäuser: 2000.

Merrick, Jay. "Something new under the sun." *The Independent*, 22 August 2000.

Dyckhoff Tom. "Centres of Attraction." *Design Journal*, January 1999.

Bauman, Irena. "The Edge between Nature and Woman-made." *Drawing on Diversity* exhibition catalog, Heinz Gallery, London, 1997.

Melhuish, Clare. "Art and Architecture: The Dynamics of Collaboration." *Architectural Design*, July/August 1997.

Melvin, Jeremy. "Beside the Seaside." *RIBA Journal*, June 1997.

FIRM PROFILE

Bauman Lyons is committed to working with and contributing to the local community and environment. A small and cohesive team, it is motivated by the challenges presented by each client and the desire to achieve innovative design solutions. The firm's project list ranges from museums and galleries to housing, offices, restaurants and bars, exhibition and urban design, and collaborative installations.

We like to experiment with the collaborative process of design, and in the past few years have worked with artists, sculptors, writers, graphic designers, and photographers on a variety of schemes. Inclusion of artists in a traditional architectural team frees up the design process from the temptation to rely on standard and tested solutions. It encourages extensive investigation, resulting in more thoroughly examined and original designs.

Although we work within a strategic framework for each project, and rely on a sense of the overall process of the design itself, we never lose sight of the project's individual details. Project management skills within the practice enable us to manage large schemes and complex teams, with detailed knowledge of funding systems, business planning, programming, risk assessment, and cost control, yet we pay as much attention to fine detail in design as we do to strategic overview and the process of the design itself.

Selected Clients

East Riding of Yorkshire Council
Kirklees Metropolitan Council
Leeds City Council
National Museum of Photography, Film and Television Gallery
Unity Housing Association
Yorkshire Sculpture Park

DESIGN STATEMENT

In 1996, Bauman Lyons was commissioned to refurbish Bridlington Promenade, a one-mile long promenade in the small seaside town of Bridlington, located in the East Riding of Yorkshire, on the North Sea.

Our commission called for a new approach to promenade design in a town that was architecturally undistinguished. One of the aims of the project was to "turn the economic tide" of a small seaside town's declining economy, yet the location—the edge between nature and man-made—required that we

investigate how to insert new man-made elements into the landscape to enhance it and not, as is often the case, to deface it.

Later in the design process, further challenges were encountered, such as the need for privacy within an essentially public space and how to recognize and respect the increasingly wild and contemplative nature of the promenade toward its south end. In our design, we developed "private" spaces within the public realm, with water channels and thirty individual bridges serving each chalet and defining its private space. We also created a gradient of intensity, concentrating most of the intense activities on the north end and then gradually reducing the provisions as the promenade moves south. The exception is the Headland Café, built into the cliff at the south end, acting as a discreet destination for those prepared to walk the full nautical mile to the end.

When designing the individual elements of the scheme—a commercial site containing a café, shops, terraces, and a deck chair store; chalets; two toilet blocks; the Headland Café; the paddling pool; and the beach watch office—we had to develop an architectural language that was fresh and contemporary but still acknowledged the influence of traditional forms associated with seaside architecture.

The greatest challenge in the process was our design collaboration with the artist, Bruce McLean. As in all collaborations, the benefits—innovation and quality of ideas—were significant, but different styles of operation and levels of responsibility and involvement led, at times, to conflicts that had to be resolved as the project progressed.

Ultimately, the completed project achieved its aims through the collaboration of an enlightened client, an innovative and responsible design team, and an open-minded community.

ILLUSTRATED PROJECTS

Refurbishment of South Promenade, Bridlington, UK, 1996–1998

Models for proposed public space, Garston, Liverpool, UK, completion due March 2001

Media Center, Leeds, UK, completion due May 2001

Chinese Community Center, Leeds, UK, 1997

Refurbishment of South Promenade, Bridlington, UK: 1 View from the chalets across the water channel and bridges in the middle section of the promenade; 2 The busy north end of the promenade on a hot day; 3 New chalets designed as a "contemporary take on a traditional theme," with timber bridges defining the private territory of each chalet. Pitched roofs and the use of timber acknowledge the vernacular tradition; the offset ridge axis, use of glass, and detailing are contemporary interpretations. Strong colors in the interiors provide colorful backdrops to seaside activities in summer months. External colors are calm and natural to complement the quiet nature of the seaside in winter months when chalets are locked; 4 Terrace above the shops and café, designed to preserve views of the sea, offer opportunities for solitude, and evoke a strong nautical feeling; 5 Headland Café, at the south end of the promenade; 6 Detail of bay watch office, designed as a pavilion that relates to the "family" of other buildings on the promenade in terms of materials and detailing, but is distinct in form. The strong roof form was devised to provide good visibility as it is used by visitors for emergencies. Photo credits: Neil Verow [2, 3]; Marine Hamilton Knight [1, 4, 6]; Martin Peters [5]

Refurbishment of South Promenade, Bridlington, UK (continued): 7 View down the row of chalets; 8 Model of a section through the promenade; 9 Detail of Headland Café, designed with artist Bruce McLean. Photo credits: Martine Hamilton Knight [7]; Martin Peters [8]; Neil Verow [9]

[Below] **Proposed Public Space, Garston, Liverpool, UK:** 1 Model of proposed performance space at east end of pedestrian zone/marketplace. Space is formed in colored concrete with text specially written for project sandblasted into the surface; 2 Detail of integrated lighting column set on 26-foot (8-m) grid; two market stalls can be suspended between columns on market days; 3 Detailed model of street bench, with bins integrated to one end. Photo credits: Michael Trigg

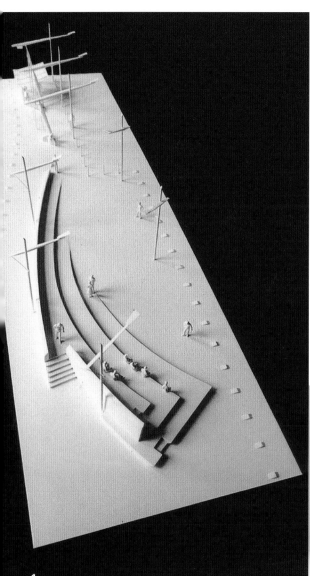

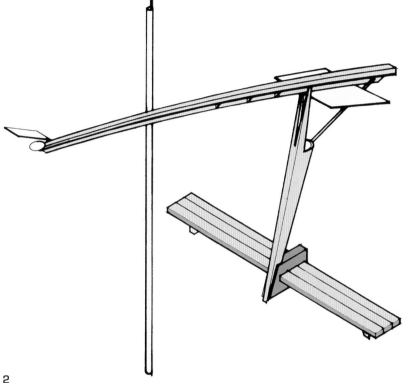

2

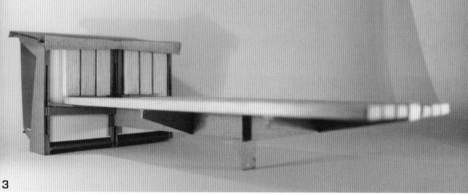

1

3

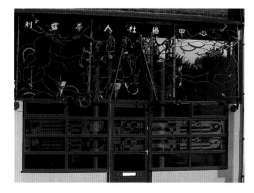

[Above] **Chinese Community Center, Leeds, UK:** Front of new center, designed in collaboration with artist Madeline Miller. Design is based on Chinese motifs, with metalwork made by using scrap materials. Photo credit: Ian Beesley

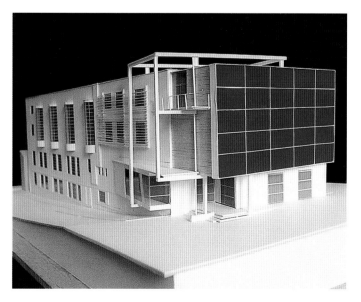

[Left] **Media Center, Leeds, UK:** Model showing extension to facility for creative industries. Design is strong and contemporary to emphasize new energy in neighborhood. Photo credit: Michael Trigg

Ann Beha
United States of America

"When I design, I start by looking, and by listening. I am listening for the client's mission and dreams, and the way that the client perceives itself. I am looking at the site or building, its setting, and its community. Looking and listening fuels me creatively and frees me to make a building unique and purposeful."

PROFESSIONAL HISTORY

Ann Macy Beha received a bachelor of arts degree from Wellesley College in 1972 and a master's degree in architecture from the Massachusetts Institute of Technology (MIT) in 1975. From 1975 to 1977 she was assistant to the head of the Department of Architecture at MIT, and in 1977 and 1978 she was a research associate, also at MIT. In 1977–78, she founded and became president of Ann Beha Associates, Inc.

In 1987–88, Beha was awarded a Loeb Fellowship in Environmental Design at the Harvard Graduate School of Design, and in 1998 was named a fellow of the American Institute of Architects (AIA). From 1989 to 2000, she was a trustee of the Society for the Preservation of New England Antiquities. Beha has also served on numerous committees and advisory boards, including the Visiting Committee of the School of Architecture and Planning at MIT and three visiting committees for departments of the Boston Museum of Fine Arts: European Decorative Arts and Sculpture, American Decorative Arts and Sculpture, and Research and Objects Conservation. She is a member of the Honors and Awards Committee of the Boston Society of Architects and an advisory board member for Historic Massachusetts Inc., a statewide preservation organization based in Boston.

Selected Awards

Alumnae Achievement Award, Wellesley College, 1999

Boston Society of Architects Design Award, 1997

Lifetime Achievement Award, Victorian Society of America, New England Chapter, 1994

American Wood Council Merit Award, 1989

25th Anniversary Preservation Award, Massachusetts Historical Commission, 1988

Governor's Design Award, Commonwealth of Massachusetts, Region III, 1986

Tucker Award for Design Excellence, Building Stone Institute, 1985 and 1986

Selected Publications

Busch, Jennifer Thiele. "There Once Was a Place in Nantucket." *Contract*, March 2000.

"Ann with a Plan." *The Hilltopper: Worcester Academy Magazine*, Summer 1999.

Beha, Ann. "The Museum Challenge." *The Construction Specifier*, November 1998.

Randall, Kathleen. "Wit and Wisdom at Work." *Traditional Building*, September 1998.

"Revising Belluschi." *Architecture*, November 1996.

Linn, Charles. "A Classical Hall Played Lightly." *Architectural Record Lighting*, February 1996.

Kahn, Eve M. "Transmuting History." *Traditional Building*, September 1993.

FIRM PROFILE

Ann Beha Associates (ABA) designs for culture and community. Over the past twenty-two years, ABA has achieved broad recognition for its designs for museums, libraries, theaters, religious facilities, and educational environments, which successfully embrace change while respecting historical settings. The firm's decades of experience on preservation projects enrich its mastery of materials, craft, and technology. This knowledge is now also widely applied to original design work for contemporary structures.

ABA believes that the building design must reflect a collective vision as well as further a client's mission. Clients, artists, and users participate in the design process, and the design vision draws from these sources. Design solutions are judged not only for their aesthetics, but also by the degree to which they meet an institution's needs for change and growth.

ABA's passion for history and its commitment to innovative and enduring structures attracts a staff of talented professionals. Together they have expanded the firm's influence, both in preserving the past and in creating architecture for future generations.

Selected Clients

Boston Symphony Orchestra

Brown University, *Providence, Rhode Island*

The First Church of Christ, Scientist, *Boston, Massachusetts*

The Isabella Stewart Gardner Museum, *Boston, Massachusetts*

The Metropolitan Museum of Art, *New York City*

The National Trust for Historic Preservation

The New England Conservatory of Music, *Boston, Massachusetts*

The Portland Art Museum, *Portland, Oregon*

The Taft Museum, *Cincinnati, Ohio*

Wellesley College, *Wellesley, Massachusetts*

The Worcester Art Museum, *Worcester, Massachusetts*

DESIGN STATEMENT

Architecture captures the spirit of change, but is also bound by its time. How can design be made timeless, serving the future and not just its moment? I welcome projects that bring time and change together.

ABA works with nonprofit clients, both in historic settings and in environmentally sensitive sites, to design timeless and innovative architecture. In all of our projects, the challenge is to establish links between old and new, developing an architectural framework that brings an existing building or site into vigorous dialogue with the future. At the Portland Art Museum in Oregon, we renovated and expanded three buildings originally by Belluschi, joining them as one art museum with collections spanning centuries and incorporating many cultures. At Franklin and Marshall College, in Pennsylvania, we viewed a 1930s academic building, Hensel Hall, as a setting, and installed a new environment for music, film, and community.

With each design, our approach is unique. At the Portland Museum, light is a guiding element—overhead, as a vista, as a lantern—drawing visitors through galleries and civic spaces. At Hensel Hall, light is controlled and modulated to enhance the audience's connection to the performers. Our work for performing arts insists that the interface between architecture and acoustics is seamless. Materials are warm and rich at Hensel, strongly contrasting and intended to wrap the audience into the space, to focus them on the music. At Portland, materials are light, serene, luring the visitor through the galleries, up, around, and toward the works of art. The museum's palette is distinct to the Northwest: natural woods and stone, soft and simple as a setting for art and for social and community life.

These are solutions that draw inspiration from the traditions of each place and the client's aspirations. The intention is to engage, to delight the visitor with a play of old and new, light and dark, simplicity and complexity. This is true of my work and is reflected in the projects of our entire team.

ILLUSTRATED PROJECTS

Portland Art Museum, Portland, Oregon, 1996–2000

Hensel-Barshinger Concert Hall, Franklin & Marshall College, Lancaster, Pennsylvania, 1999

[Opposite] **Portland Art Museum, Portland, Oregon:** 1 1932 building by Pietro Belluschi, renovated by ABA; 2 Auditorium and film theater below sculpture court; 3 Renovated gallery in original building. Photo credit: Hewitt/Garrison Architectural Photography

[Below] **Hensel-Barshinger Concert Hall, Franklin & Marshall College, Lancaster, Pennsylvania:** 1 View of orchestra level of new concert hall; 2 View from stage to audience; 3 View to stage from balcony. Photo credit: Tom Crane Architectural Photography

Caroline Bos
The Netherlands

Photo credit: Menno Kok

"The architect is going to be the fashion designer of the future. Learning from designers like Calvin Klein, the architect will be concerned with dressing the future—speculating, anticipating coming events, and holding a mirror to the world."

PROFESSIONAL HISTORY

Caroline Bos received a bachelor of arts in art history from Birkbeck College, University of London in 1991. In 1988, she founded Van Berkel & Bos in Amsterdam with architect Ben van Berkel. Van Berkel & Bos has designed several critically acclaimed projects, including the Karbouw offices and Villa Wilbrink in Amersfoort, the Netherlands; the Erasmus Bridge in Rotterdam; the Möbius-house in 't Gooi, just outside Amsterdam; and Museum Het Valkhof in Nijmegen.

In recent years, Van Berkel & Bos has focused on new planning strategies and organizational structures. Current projects include a master plan for the center of Arnhem, the Netherlands; an electricity station in Innsbruck, Austria; a laboratory in Utrecht, the Netherlands; and a music theater in Graz, Austria.

In 1998, Ben van Berkel and Caroline Bos established UN Studio, a network of specialists in architecture, urban development, and infrastructure. The two organizations are now combined as UN Studio Van Berkel & Bos, based in Amsterdam.

In addition to her work as an architect and builder, Bos participates in international exhibitions, writes, and has lectured and taught at various architectural schools. At present she is a thesis tutor at the Berlage Institute in Amsterdam, which offers a postgraduate curriculum in architecture, urban planning, and landscape architecture.

Selected Awards: UN Studio Van Berkel & Bos

Winning entry for Papendorp Bridge, Utrecht, the Netherlands 1998

Winning entry for Music Theater, Graz, Austria 1998

Winning entry for Electricity Station, Innsbruck, Austria 1997

Winning entry for Museum Het Valkhof, Nijmegen, the Netherlands 1995

Winning entry for the police headquarters in Berlin Köpenick, 1995

Charlotte Köhler Prize, 1991

Selected Publications

van Berkel, Ben and Caroline Bos. *MOVE*. Monograph. Amsterdam: Goose Press, 1999.

van Berkel, Ben and Caroline Bos. *Museum Het Valkhof*. Amsterdam: UN Studio, 1999.

Sowa, Axel, ed. "UN Studio." *L'Architecture d'Aujourd'hui*, March 1999.

van Berkel, Ben. *Mobile Forces*. Monograph. Berlin: Ernst & Sohn, 1994.

van Berkel, Ben and Caroline Bos. *Delinquent Visionaries*. Rotterdam: 010 Publishers, 1993, 1994.

FIRM PROFILE: UN STUDIO

Established in 1998, UN Studio organizes strategic forms of collaboration with architects, graphic designers, building consultants, service companies, quantity surveyors, and other specialists. Connectivity is the key concept. Based in Amsterdam, UN Studio has an international orientation.

UN Studio is not only a design studio but also handles technical details and project supervision. Internal teams, including a design team, management team, coordination team, and technology team, are supplemented with specialist know-how from external organizations. Computer technology makes it possible to combine early-stage design concepts with research on details.

UN Studio works on a wide range of projects, from small- to large-scale public network projects. The objective is to utilize intensive forms of collaboration to carry out ambitious building projects that will serve as influential nodes. Bos and van Berkel refer to their overall approach to urban design as *deep planning*, which involves exhaustive analysis of the overall context in which buildings will be situated. The postindustrial city is not a collection of discrete units, but a nodal network, connected not only by increasingly complex lines of communication but by mutual dependence on a variety of parameters that necessarily change over time, such as social, economic, and political conditions, infrastructure, and stages of construction. If planning takes into account only data on individual components, no matter how accurate the data is, the process is flawed. The analysis of relations, over time, is key to generating current designs that will be viable in the future.

Selected Clients: UN Studio Van Berkel & Bos

Amt der Steiermärkischen Landesregierung, *Graz, Austria*

City of Arnhem, *the Netherlands*

Holland Railconsult, *Utrecht, the Netherlands*

Innsbrucker Kommunalbetriebe AG (IKB), *Innsbruck, Austria*

Landesbaudirektion, *Graz, Austria*

Museum Het Valkhof, *Nijmegen, the Netherlands*

Projectbureau Leidsche Rijn, *Utrecht, the Netherlands*

Randstad Dienstengroep Nederland b.v., *Amsterdam*

University of Utrecht, Bijvoet Institute, *Utrecht, the Netherlands*

DESIGN STATEMENT

Rather than describe a specific project, Caroline Bos chose to make a theoretical statement based on her monograph, MOVE, *which documents the buildings and designs developed by UN Studio Van Berkel & Bos between 1994 and 1999.*

The architectural production that provided the foundation for the book *MOVE* took place over a period of five years, from 1994 to 1999. At the heart of the book are two questions and three related topics. The first question concerns how to express the global imagination in contemporary organizational structures; the second, how to incorporate current theories concerning the planning and mediation of public space into contemporary architectural effects. The three topics concern the ways in which the three enduring ingredients of architecture—the creative imagination, techniques, and effects—are expressed in the built environment today.

MOVE is an attempt to reconnect theory and technique, imagination and practice. It examines the new role of the architect in the context of changing patterns in our postindustrial, global societies and the ways in which the architect might respond to these changes. It is also about redefining organizational structures at every level. Organizational structures should not be modeled on homogeneous, linear systems, but seen as evolving forms subject to expansion, contraction, inversion, and almost endless variation.

MOVE, and the work of UN Studio Van Berkel & Bos, focuses on an inclusive design approach—an integration of program, construction methods, and the needs of clients and the surrounding community. Inclusiveness abandons fragmentation, yet at the same time embraces difference. The design process is coherent and continuous.

ILLUSTRATED PROJECT

Museum Het Valkhof, Nijmegen, the Netherlands, 1999: Two main structures organize the museum: the staircase and the undulating ceiling. The museum floor is divided into parallel "streets" with multiple lateral openings; attracted by light or cross-views through the streets, visitors follow their own individual routes.

Museum Het Valkhof, Nijmegen, the Netherlands: 1 Exterior; 2&3 Exhibition room. Public, administrative, and storage functions are housed on the ground floor, while museum and exhibition spaces occupy the first floor; 4 Gallery; 5 Another exterior angle; 6 Section plan; 7&8 Gallery. Like a blanket casually thrown over an object, the ceiling covers, but does not conceal or disguise, lighting and climate control installations, wires, fixings and fittings, sprinklers, and alarms; 9 The staircase is the structural core of the building and is also a distributor—its branches shoot off to the various program parts, such as the café, library, museum, and central hall; 10 Site plan. Photo credit: Remco Bruggink; Christian Richters.

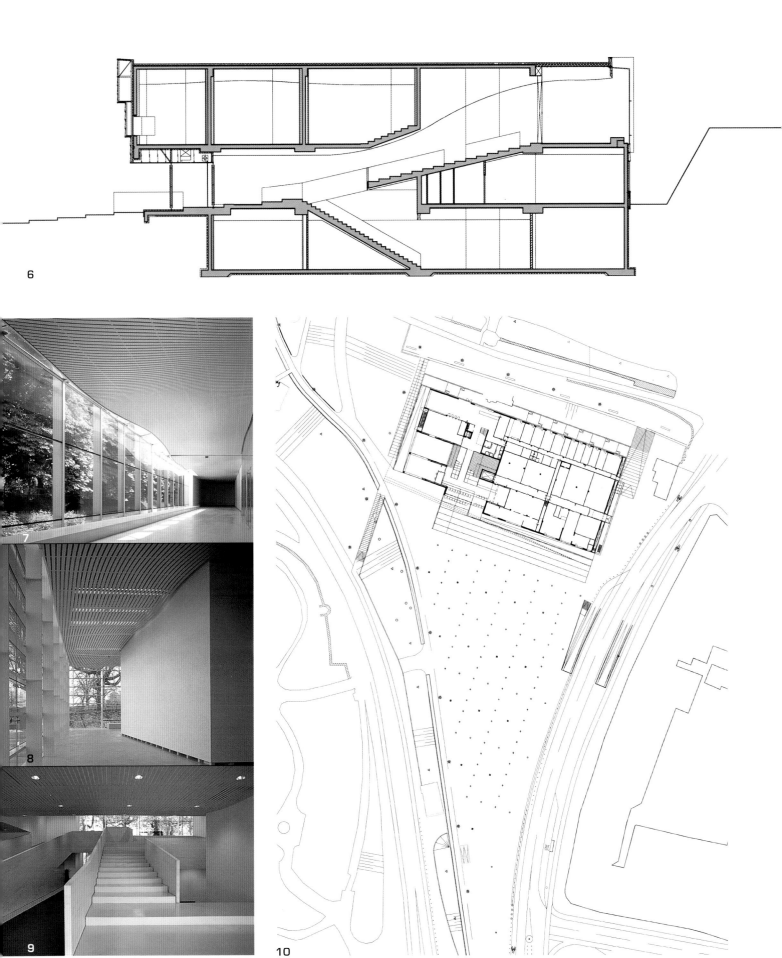

6

7

8

9

10

Alison Brooks

United Kingdom

"I like it when we break the 'rules' we set up for ourselves in the previous project, or in the last five projects. Suddenly you can be self-critical and move on, make progress. Then we know we aren't falling into an ideological or conceptual trap that could make the work formulaic, identifiable. I don't want to get caught up in the boy's-digital-technological fetish. That whole blob-obsessed scene has already become the establishment—the auto-didactic international style of the new millennium."

PROFESSIONAL HISTORY

Alison Brooks received a bachelor's degree in architecture from the University of Waterloo School of Architecture in Canada in 1988. While a student, she also gained practical experience in several well-known firms, including A. J. Diamond & Partners, where she worked on several landmark Toronto buildings.

In 1989, Brooks relocated to London to work with Ron Arad in developing a design for the Tel Aviv Opera competition. In 1991, she became a founding partner in Ron Arad Associates, where she was jointly responsible for several award-winning works, including the Tel Aviv Opera foyer and the renowned London restaurants Belgo Noord and Belgo Centraal.

In 1996, Brooks founded Alison Brooks Architects in North London. Since then, her ability to challenge parameters has resulted in a string of award-winning hotel, urban design, and housing schemes in Germany and Britain.

Selected Awards

Winner, European Hotel Design and Development Awards 2000. First prize overall hotel design and best guestroom and bathroom. Shortlisted, Hurlingham Park Sports Pavilion in Hammersmith, England

Runner-up, Europan 5 International Housing Design Competition, for "Airscape" in Harlemermeer, the Netherlands, 1999

Second Prize, *Daily Mail*/International Concept House Competition, for a prototype terrace house for the future, 1999

Third Prize, BD/British Steel Young Architect of the Year Award, 1999

Winner, Liverpool RopeWalks Street Furniture Competition, for free-form street furniture design, 1999

Architectural Review Prize, for Tel Aviv Opera Foyer, jointly with Rod Arad, 1994

Selected Publications

"Hotel Atoll–Helgoland, Almania." *Diseno Interior*, November 2000.

"Hotel Atoll Helgoland." *Elle Deco*, May 2000.

"Submarine Dream." *Architectural Review*, March 2000.

"Europan 5." Hoogewoning, Anne and Emmie Vos, eds. Rotterdam: Nai Uitgevers Publishers, 1999.

Perrella, Stephen, guest ed. *Hypersurface Architecture II*. Chichester, West Sussex: Academy Editions, 1999.

Scheuermann, Rudi and Keith Boxer. *Tensile Architecture in the Urban Context*. Oxford; Boston: Butterworth-Heinemann, 1996.

FIRM PROFILE

Alison Brooks Architects (ABA) is a young, multifaceted architecture and design practice based in Islington, London. Founded in 1996, it is recognized for producing work that crosses the artificial boundaries of design convention. With a design process open to cross-fertilization with nonarchitectural and sensory worlds, every project is born from a fertile mulch of ideas that maximize the idiosyncrasies, and expand the potential of, the project brief. Movement, sensation, and idea rebound to create an accessible architecture with direct impact on quality of life.

ABA's projects encompass urban design and landscapes, public and commercial buildings, housing, private residential work, brand concepts, and products. In 1999, the practice completed the Atoll Hotel on the German island of Helgoland, producing the brand concept and all interiors and elements of the building, including a 120-seat cafe, ninety-seat restaurant, bar, conference rooms, pool, health club, forty-two guest rooms, and furniture (currently in development for commercial production). ABA recently won an international competition to design site-specific street furniture for the RopeWalks area of Liverpool, and was shortlisted for an open competition to design the new Hurlingham Park Sports Pavilion in Hammersmith, England. Current projects include two large private residences and a landscape in a Hampstead conservation area, and a two-story warehouse conversion in Islington (both in England).

DESIGN STATEMENT

Emotion, sensation, instinct, and fantasy propel ideas outside precedent—outside the emotional straightjacket of the architectural world.

ABA produces work that is intensely site- and brief-specific, particular, and idiosyncratic. This is a good way to avoid repeating solutions or becoming stylistically entrenched: by deriving solutions from the real experiences of a situation ("site-uation"). The project becomes a collaboration of discovered desires, accessible and readable, open to invention. The design problem is re-framed, or "un-framed." Unplanned complexities (or simplicities) emerge and invite discovery. Within this "un-framework," humor and playfulness slide into the work, humor being an emotion that reaches across boundaries of role, status, and expectation.

Much of the most inventive architecture today happens at the level of commercial interiors. People don't pay to go sit in a new housing development and be entertained by the scenery. But they do pay to sit in a restaurant, to overindulge their senses and be steeped in clever design at every level. ABA looks forward to the day when the inventiveness and unadulterated pleasure of restaurant design hits the streets—a new vision for (sub)urban living and infrastructure, based on pure physical pleasure and unexpected playfulness.

ILLUSTRATED PROJECTS

Atoll Helgoland Hotel, Helgoland, Germany, 1999: This commission for a hotel on the island of Helgoland, Germany included a total design solution for the hotel interiors and buildings. The owner's man-made atoll, a circular steel vessel formerly used as a deep-sea diving platform, was ABA's inspiration for the hotel brand and a metaphor for the interior concept—a smooth "liquid" space inhabited by a new species of tactile plastic forms.

V-house, London: A 3,000-square-foot conversion of a 1960s Hamstead family house; the extension is a 1,070-square-foot timber-clad cube supported on one V. Below the cube is a glazed foyer masquerading as a covered outdoor patio. Integral to the space is a screen wall that is a canvas for a specially commissioned wall drawing by artist Simon Patterson.

Soundscape, Hammersmith, UK, currently obtaining funding: This scheme creates a 500-meter-long sine-wave earthwork and new public park on the site of a derelict square in Hammersmith. The scheme was produced after extensive public consultation and design workshops in the local community.

Airscape, Europan 5, Haarlemmermeer, the Netherlands, 1998: New housing elevated onto platforms six meters above a public park. A structural lattice allows housing to be sold as cubic meters of airspace.

Urban DNA Housing, Manchester, UK, 1999: A new housing prototype that exploits fast-track construction systems, economies of scale, and the urban character of a brownfield site to provide flexible, low-cost urban lofts.

FUL House, concept design, 1999: Prototype terraced housing for the future. Curved party walls provide 26-feet-wide open-plan spaces.

Atoll Helgoland Hotel, Helgoland, Germany: 1 Bar; 2 View of a bedroom; 3 View of the bistro stairway; 4 View of restaurant banquets against a wall clad in aluminum and noise-dampening fabrics; 5 View of the swimming pool, looking down one of the massive cones projecting into the pool ceiling from hotel lobby above; 6 Reception; 7 View of the bistro, showing a hole in the floor that leads through to the pool; 8 Ground floor plan. Photo credit: courtesy Christoph Kicherer

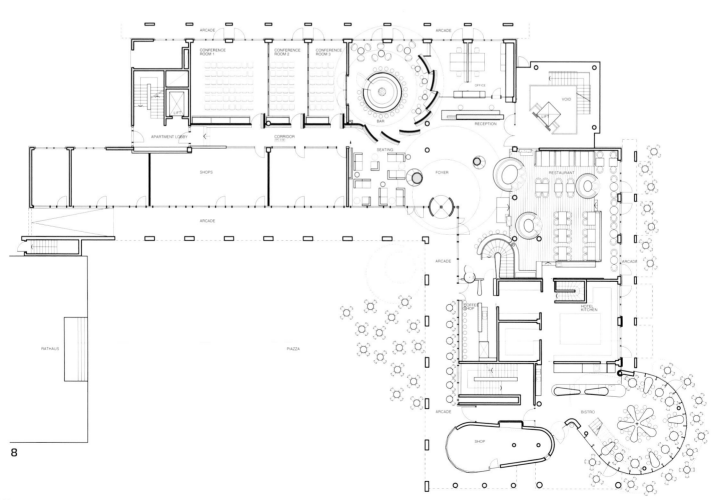

V-house, London: 1 Floor plans (before on left and after on right); 2 Etched door; 3 Computer model of nighttime exterior view showing glazed foyer and outdoor patio; 4 Interior showing suspended staircase; 5 Computer model of nighttime exterior view showing glazed foyer, wall drawing by Simon Patterson; 6 Daytime exterior view. Photo credit: courtesy Alison Brooks Architects

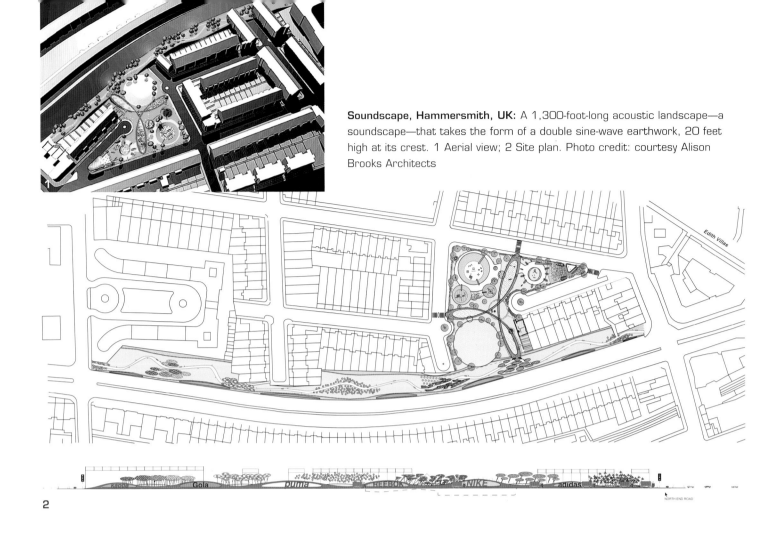

Soundscape, Hammersmith, UK: A 1,300-foot-long acoustic landscape—a soundscape—that takes the form of a double sine-wave earthwork, 20 feet high at its crest. 1 Aerial view; 2 Site plan. Photo credit: courtesy Alison Brooks Architects

2

[Above] **Airscape, Europan 5, Haarlemmermeer, the Netherlands:** Proposal for the development of an extremely flat, isolated island site. The potentially extreme suburban conditions are counteracted by elevating the housing units and designating the entire site a public park. Photo credit: courtesy Alison Brooks Architects

[Below] **Urban DNA Housing, Manchester, UK:** [1–3] Housing prototypes. Photo credit: courtesy Alison Brooks Architects

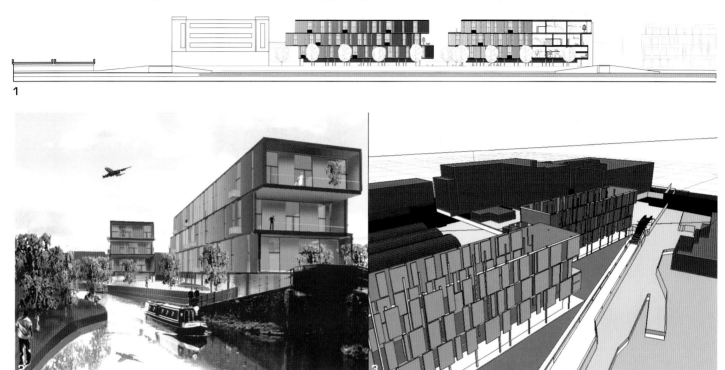

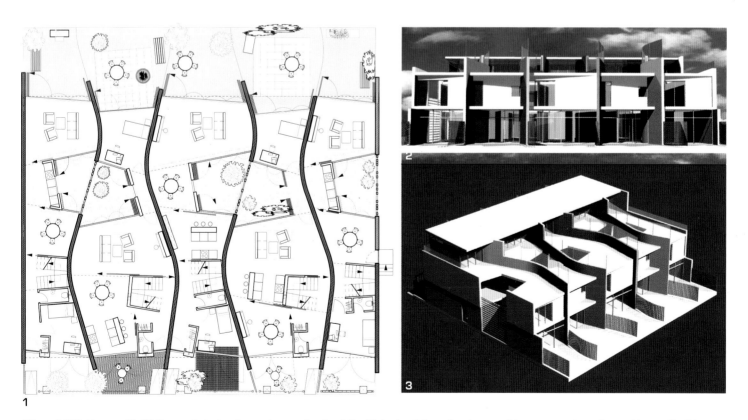

[Above] **FUL House:** [1–3] Concept design for metamorphosis of the Victorian-Edwardian terraced house, now transformed into a flexible, climate-responsive social habitat for future urban life. Series of zones allows for private, semi-public, and public spaces according to the occupants' desires. Natural light is brought deep into the house via a courtyard with a retractable translucent membrane that retains heat in winter and induces cross-ventilation in summer. Photo credit: courtesy Alison Brooks Architects

Lise Anne Couture

United States of America

*"Architecture is as much about difference—even irreconcilability—as it
is about alignment and convergence. It is a complex field of dynamic,
fluctuating relationships."*

PROFESSIONAL HISTORY

Lise Anne Couture graduated from Carleton College in 1983 and received a master's of architecture from Yale University in 1986. In 1988 she co-founded Asymptote Architecture with Hani Rashid in New York City.

Couture has held visiting professor appointments at numerous academic institutions, including the University of Montreal; the Berlag Institute, Amsterdam; Harvard University's Graduate School of Design; Barnard College; Columbia University's Graduate School of Architecture, Preservation, and Planning; and Parsons School of Design in New York City.

In 1992 she was awarded a fellowship by the New York Foundation for the Arts; in 1995 she was named to the New York City area's "40 under 40" list; and in 1999 she was selected by the Architectural League of New York as an "Emerging Voice."

Selected Awards: Asymptote

First prize, Los Angeles West Coast Gateway, a building commemorating Pacific Rim immigration

First prize, National Courthouse, Groningen, the Netherlands (with Wielarets Assoc.)

Fourth prize, library in Alexandria, Egypt

Honorable mention, Moscow State Theater

Selected Publications

Ho, Cathy. "Computer Power." *Architecture*, May 2000.

Amelar, Sarah. "Asymptote's Dual Projects for the New York Stock Exchange." *Architectural Record*, June 1999.

"Asymptote: Rashid + Couture." *Architecture + Urbanism*, no. 344, 1999.

Pearson, Clifford and Suzanne Stephen. "Asymptote Envisions a Sleek and Dynamic Museum of Technology Culture." *Architectural Record*, December 1999.

Couture, Lise Anne and Hani Rashid. *Asymptote: Rashid + Couture*. Monograph. New York: Rizzoli International, 1995.

"Lise Anne Couture." *Architecture + Urbanism*, Japan, December 1989.

FIRM PROFILE

Asymptote is an internationally recognized design firm based in New York City. From the outset, co-founding architects Hani Rashid and Lise Anne Couture conceived of Asymptote as a collaborative, multidisciplinary undertaking.

For over a decade, they have experimented with various types of media, such as collage, photographic techniques, and digital technology, and their work encompasses a wide range of project types, including residential buildings, corporate centers, interior design, furniture, and urban design, as well as multimedia installation art and, most recently, interactive digital environments. As technology has evolved over the course of their practice, Rashid and Couture have sought to embrace its creative potential while intellectually and architecturally investigating its cultural and spatial implications.

Public building projects by Asymptote include a cultural center in Tours, France; a music theater in Graz, Austria; a museum of modern art in Aarhus, Denmark; the National Museum in Seoul, Korea; a new parliamentary precinct for Berlin; a historical museum in Tohoku, and a passenger ship terminal in Yokohama, both located in Japan. Other clients of note are Kyoto Research Park and Knoll International. Asymptote's evolving interest in digital technologies was the focus of some recent high-profile projects, including the command center on the New York Stock Exchange Trading floor and the Guggenheim Virtual Museum in New York City, a World Wide Web-based, interactive museum that should be up and running by early 2001. The virtual trading center, 3DTF (for "three-dimensional trading floor"), features state-of-the-art technology and allows traders both to navigate within a virtual landscape and to check on remote operations without leaving the trading floor.

Asymptote's work is included in the collections of the Museum of Modern Art in New York, the San Francisco Museum of Modern Art, the Canadian Center for Architecture in Montreal, and the Fond Regionale d'Art Contemporain du Centre in Orléans, France, as well as in several private collections. Their projects have been widely exhibited, including venues in Paris, Frankfurt, Berlin, Vienna, London, Kyoto, Montreal, Toronto, San Francisco, and Los Angeles.

DESIGN STATEMENT

Defined as parallel lines that meet at infinity, the name Asymptote *reflects the philosophical underpinnings of Lise Anne Couture and Hani Rashid's practice.*

The lines of the asymptote, which constantly approach each other but never touch, capture the spirit of an open-ended practice, a perpetual work in progress, where each individual project is part of a much larger body of work.

For Couture and Rashid, architecture is as much about irreconcilability and difference as it is about alignment and convergence. It is a complex field of dynamic and fluctuating relationships. Like asymptotic lines, the many simultaneous pursuits in their practice do not merge entirely but are rather like trajectories, which form an increasingly dense and rich territory for Couture and Rashid's architectural explorations.

ILLUSTRATED PROJECTS

Kyoto Research Park (KRP), Kyoto, Japan, 1997: Asymptote had stiff competition for the commission to design the core buildings for KRP, the largest private urban science and research center in Japan.

Univers Theater, Denmark, 1999: This 30,000-square-foot multimedia center occupied the central square of Aarhus between August 27 and September 5, 1999. (The Univers structure is constructed annually as the centerpiece of the Aarhus Festival, one of the most widely attended cultural celebrations in Europe.)

New York Stock Exchange Advanced Trading Floor Command Center, 1999: The virtual trading center features state-of-the-art technology and allows traders both to navigate within a virtual landscape and to check on remote operations without leaving the trading floor.

Kyoto Research Park, Kyoto, Japan: 1 Kyoto Tech Museum elevation; 2 Interior view of Entertainment and Media Center. Photo credit: courtesy Asymptote Architecture

1

2

Univers Theater, Aarhus, Denmark: 1 Night view of theater; 2 Computer rendering, top view; 3–5 Night views of theater.
Photo credit: courtesy Asymptote Architecture

New York Stock Exchange, New York City: 1&2 Trading Floor Command Center. Photo credit: courtesy Asymptote Architecture

Odile Decq
France

"Space is not only a volume—you can't open a door and understand a space in one view. We are interested in what you discover along a walk through the space."

PROFESSIONAL HISTORY AND FIRM PROFILE

Odile Decq began her architectural studies in 1971 at the School of Architecture in Rennes. In 1973 she enrolled at the University of Paris School of Architecture at La Vilette, then the most experimental of France's schools of architecture. She graduated from the University of Paris in 1978 with a diploma in architecture, and in 1979 received a diploma in urbanism and planning from the Institute of Political Studies in Paris. In the mid-1970s she also worked as an assistant to architect Phillippe Boudon, and in the late 1970s she ran her own practice, concentrating on interior design projects.

Over the last two decades, Decq has taught at various national and international academic institutions; her appointments include the following: visiting professor, University of Montreal, 1992–present; guest professor, Vienna University of Technology, 1991; and visiting professor, Grenoble School of Architecture, 1991. She has also taught at the Ecole Spéciale d'Architecture in Paris since 1992 and at the Bartlett School of Architecture at University College, London, from 1999 to 2000. Decq served as a Diploma Jury Member at both the Westminster University School of Architecture, London (1994–1999), and the Bartlett School of Architecture (1994–1999).

In 1982, Decq and Benoît Cornette co-founded Odile Decq Benoît Cornette Architects, setting up their office and studios in the Marais quarter of Paris. From 1982 until November 1998, when Benoît Cornette was killed in an automobile accident, the two worked together on numerous important and ground-breaking projects, including the Banque Populaire de l'Ouest in Rennes (1988–1990), which was the first metal-construction office building to be built in France and which won ten prizes, both national and international. Their work encompassed a broad range of project types, from the School of Economics Sciences and Law Library at the University of Nantes (1991), which cost less to build per square meter than any other university construction during the same period, to the mammoth (400 hectare [988 acre]) Gennevilliers docks commission.

Model building played a crucial role in the planning process for all Decq-Cornette projects. The first step was to constuct colored study models using modular components, which could be moved around easily. They then tested the feasibility of the various possible configurations and, last, prepared a final model for submission to jury or client. They regarded each project as a unique undertaking, analyzing its programmatic, constructional, and contextural requirements in a process that Cornette, who was training to be a doctor before he switched to architecture, likened to the process of medical diagnosis and treatment. In the preface to Clare Melhuish's book on the firm's work (see Selected Publications), Frédérick Migayro, from the French Ministry of Culture at Orléans, wrote that Decq and Cornette were among a small but important international group of architects "committed to a serious questioning of the architectural status quo and pushing the discipline to its conceptual limits."

Selected Awards: Odile Decq Benoît Cornette Architects

Benedictus Award, International Union of Architects/American Institute of Architects: School of Economics Sciences and Law Library, University of Nantes, 1999; Banque Populaire de l'Quest, Rennes, 1994

The Golden Lion, Architecture Biennale, Venice, 1996

Oscar du Design, Le Nouvel Economiste, Paris 1992

Prix, Plus Beaux Ouvrages de Construction Metallique, USINOR, Paris 1992

Premier Award, Ninth International Prize for Architecture, London 1990

Prix, Architecture et Lieux de Travail, Paris 1990

Selected Publications

Slavid, Ruth. "Displacing the Grid." *Architect's Journal*, February 1998.

Melhuish, Clare. *Odile Decq, Benoît Cornette*. London: Phaidon, 1996.

Aedes Gallery Exhibition, Berlin, Monograph, 1995.

Selected Clients

Air in Bruxelles
Banque Populaire de l'Ouest
Glass Research Center of Saint Gobain
Orléans Rugby Stadium
University of Nantes

DESIGN STATEMENT

School of Economics Sciences and Law Library, University of Nantes, France

One of the major challenges on this project was to achieve a set of complex conceptual goals while working within a limited budget. The design solutions—the use of everyday building materials, primarily anthracite zinc and laminated glass, and simple, boxlike volumes—were cost-effective and at the same time addressed long-term maintenance concerns. The glass also permitted us to create visual links between the buildings themselves and between the buildings and the green woods along the river.

ILLUSTRATED PROJECTS

Banque Populaire de l'Ouest, Rennes, France

A Third City Bridge, Rotterdam, Germany

University of Nantes, Nantes, France

Siemp Housing, Paris

Motorway Bridge, Nanterre, France

Hyper Tension Expo, Magasin Grenoble, Grenoble, France

Banque Populaire de l'Ouest,
Rennes, France
Photo credit: S. Couturior

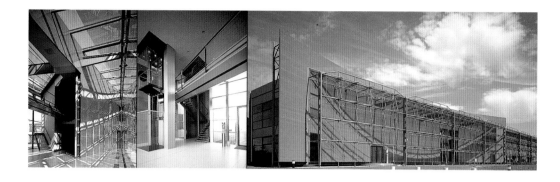

A Third City Bridge, Rotterdam,
Germany Photo credit: courtesy
of Odile Decq Benoît Cornette

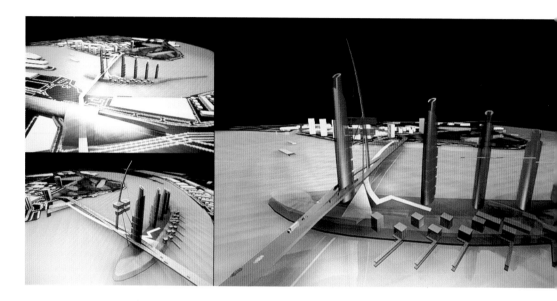

University of Nantes, Nantes, France: 1 Interior view, School
of Economics Sciences; 2 Interior of glass box inserted diagonally
between different sections of the Economics Science buildings;
3 View across courtyard of Law Library, from School of Economics
Sciences; 4 Looking up stairs in School of Economics Sciences;
on each level, the brightly colored corridors serve as a reference
code. Photo credit: Georges Fessy

[Right] Siemp Housing, Paris
Photo credit: Georges Fessy

Motorway Bridge, Nanterre, France Photo credit: George Fessy

Hyper Tension Expo, Magasin Grenoble, Grenoble, France Photo credit: Georges Fessy

Elizabeth Diller
United States of America

"We have been working in the idiom of installation because we can physically realize our ideas quickly. Architecture is too slow."

PROFESSIONAL HISTORY

Elizabeth Diller received a bachelor's degree in architecture from the Cooper Union in New York City in 1979. The same year she co-founded Diller + Scofidio in New York City with Ricardo Scofidio, who received his bachelor's degree in architecture from Columbia University in 1960.

From 1982 to 1990, Diller served as an associate adjunct professor at the Cooper Union. She has served as guest and visiting professor at a number of institutions, including Harvard and Columbia universities, the University of Hawaii at Honolulu, Sci-Arc in Los Angeles, and the Architectural Association in London. Since 1990, she has taught at Princeton University, where she is now an associate professor of architecture.

Diller is on the board of directors for Storefront for Art & Architecture in New York. She has lectured and exhibited extensively around the world.

Selected Awards: Diller + Scofidio

Progressive Architecture Design Award, for Brasserie, 2000

I.D. Design Distinction in Environments, for Brasserie, 2000

Best New Design Award, James Beard Foundation, for Brasserie, 2000

Fellowship, New York Foundation for the Arts, 1999, 1989

MacArthur Foundation Fellowship, 1999 (first ever to be awarded in architecture)

MacDermott Award for Creative Achievement, Massachusetts Institute of Technology, 1999

Selected Publications

"Blur Building." *Architecture Magazine*, April 2000: 90–95.

Luscombe, Belinda. "People to Watch: Liz Diller and Ricardo Scofidio." *Time*, 14 February 2000: 85.

Muschamp, Herbert. "Exploring Space and Time in the Here and Now." *The New York Times*, Sunday, 6 February 2000.

Scanlon, Jesse. "Elizabeth Diller and Ricardo Scofidio . . . Making it Morph." *Wired*, February 2000: 152–159.

Muschamp, Herbert. "Updating the Brasserie with Pizazz." *The New York Times*, Sunday, 29 August 1999.

Diller, Elizabeth and Ricardo Scofidio. *FLESH: Architectural Probes: The Mutant Body of Architecture*. New York: Princeton Architectural Press, 1995.

Diller, Elizabeth and Ricardo Scofidio. *Back to the Front: Tourisms of War*. New York: Princeton Architectural Press, 1994.

FIRM PROFILE

Diller + Scofidio was co-founded by Elizabeth Diller and Ricardo Scofidio in 1979. The firm is a collaborative, interdisciplinary studio at the intersection of art, architecture, and the performing arts, primarily involved in thematically driven experimental work. Its broad range of project types includes permanent and temporary installations, buildings, multimedia theater, interiors, Web projects, and print. Recent projects include the Blur Building, a multimedia building on Lake Neuchâtel, Switzerland, for Swiss EXPO 2002 (see page 49); Travelogues, a permanent media installation commissioned by JFK International Airport; and the Brasserie, a redesign of a classic restaurant in the Seagram Building, New York City. Clients include the Cartier Foundation (Paris), Gallery Ma (Tokyo), the Museum of Modern Art (New York City), United Artists Complex (San Jose, California), and Walker Art Center (Minneapolis).

The work of Diller + Scofidio is in the permanent collection of the Museum of Modern Art in New York, the San Francisco Museum of Modern Art, Musée de la Mode Paris, and in many private collections.

DESIGN STATEMENT

Blur Building. Yverdon-les-Bains, Switzerland

A "cloud" hovers over Lake Neuchâtel in the small city of Yverdon-les-Bains, Switzerland, measuring 300 feet wide by 200 feet deep and rising 50 feet above the water. The cloud is made of filtered lake water shot as a fine mist through a dense array of high-pressure water nozzles integrated into a large cantilevered tensegrity structure. Unlike mist that settles over a lake and lifts after dawn, this cloud is permanent. The public can approach via a pedestrian ramp that becomes glass-enclosed as it ascends through the cloud. Upon entering, the visual and acoustical context is slowly erased until there is a near absence of sensory stimuli. Only an optical "white-out" accompanied by the "white-noise" of the mist pulse remains. Visitors proceed up the spiraling ramp and emerge, like airplanes piercing a cloud layer, to the Angel Bar at the summit.

Midway along the passage, visitors can branch off into the black-out shell at the central core. This is a dry, dark void open to the water below and defined by a circular projection screen. A central platform for 250 people is suspended within. Twelve powerful video projectors are organized radially from the center to produce an image in the round. Live cameras, as well as computer-controlled and synchronized video programs on DVD, feed the panoramic image. The video program reinterprets the nineteenth-century genre of painted panorama through a twenty-first-century filter.

The painted panorama has been typified as the first mass media phenomenon, integrating actual and illusionary space by wrapping the picture plane around the spectator. The painting provided a "total view" of a controllable world that converged at the eye of each spectator. Although the panorama gave way to new public amusements in the early twentieth century, its traces can be seen in the present-day obsession with immersion technologies, such as virtual environments and IMAX. Whether viewers find themselves on a mountaintop in a panoramic painting or clinging to the edge of a precipice in a 70 mm IMAX movie, the strategy is similar: to give the viewer a safe and sanitized vantage point inside the event.

World fairs and expositions act as markers of progress and cultural development. Since humans can no longer claim to be in the center of a controllable universe, the position of the spectator continues to be an issue for critical reflection. For this project, the theme of "progress" is both the weapon and the target. Using electronic media, the revised panorama accepts the centered observer and wrap-around view, but twists its spatial conventions to challenge geographical continuity and linear time.

ILLUSTRATED PROJECTS

Facsimile, *permanent media installation commissioned by San Francisco Public Arts Commission for Moscone Convention Center, for winter 2002*

Slither Housing, Kitagata Housing, Gifu, Japan, 2000

Blur Building, multimedia building on Lake Neuchâtel, Switzerland, for Swiss EXPO 2002

Facsimile, **San Francisco:** 1 View of the installation, showing the 27- by 16-foot video screen, suspended by a vertical structure that rides on a horizontal track. Several live video cameras are fixed along the height of the structure, pointed both into and away from the building; 2–4 The structure travels slowly along the building's facade, broadcasting live and prerecorded video imagery as it moves, the latter constructed to simulate the same speed and direction as the moving structure and live footage. The structure can be viewed as a scanning device, a magnifying lens, and an instrument of deception substituting impostors for actual building occupants and spaces. Photo credit: courtesy Diller + Scofidio. Credits: Moscone Center, San Francisco Arts Commission. Principals: Elizabeth Diller and Ricardo Scofidio; Project Leader: Lyn Rice; Engineer: Les Okregiak and Pol-X West

[Right, bottom] **Slither Housing, Kitagata Housing, Gifu, Japan:** 1 South face, showing units assembled in stacks, each interlocking with the next at a slight angle. Overlapping "scales" of perforated metal screening offer degrees of privacy in corridors and balconies;
2 The floor slab of each unit is offset vertically from the next, with a system of shallow ramps stringing the units together to create a subtle topography in which no two units share the same elevation; 3 Each unit's plan slips 4 1/2 feet (1.4 m) from the next, freeing each entry door on the north side to be approached at an axis and creating private balconies on the south side. Photo credit: courtesy Diller + Scofidio; Koji Kobayashi (1); Michael Moran (2). Principals: Elizabeth Diller and Ricardo Scofidio; Team: Paul Lewis, Project Leader, with Patrice Gardera and Matthias Hollwich

Blur Building, Yverdon-les-Bains, Switzerland: 1 Tensegrity structure of "cloud" hovering over Lake Nuechâtel; 2 Cross section at panorama; 3 Visitors approach the cloud from shore via a pedestrian ramp; 4 Artificial cloud as viewed from shore. A built-in weather station electronically adjusts water pressure and temperature at 13 zones according to shifting humidity and wind direction and speed; 5 At the top, visitors emerge through the cloud to the Angel Bar. Photo credit: courtesy Diller + Scofidio. The Blur Building is part of a larger team project with Extasia, Diller + Scofidio. Principals: Elizabeth Diller and Ricardo Scofidio; Team: Eric Bunge, Project Leader, with Karin Ocker, Alex Haw, and Charles Renfro

Julie Eizenberg
United States of America

"Architecture is an opportunity to reassess simple pleasures—light, air, view, color, and natural beauty. Consequently, I favor design strategies that highlight outside spaces and frame activities, people, and the landscape. For me, context is more accurately described as the space between buildings rather than the stylistic ornament of neighboring structures. By manipulating forms, materials, scale, light, and ornament, we make the familiar and the simple seem extraordinary."

PROFESSIONAL HISTORY

Julie Eizenberg holds degrees in architecture from the University of Melbourne, Australia, and the University of California in Los Angeles (UCLA), and is licensed as an architect in both California and Australia. In 1981 she became founding principal of Koning Eizenberg Architecture Inc., with Hendrik Koning, FAIA, FRAIA. Eizenberg currently teaches part-time at UCLA's Graduate School of Architecture and Urban Planning, and has lectured extensively in the United States and abroad.

As the firm's design principal, Eizenberg has led the design effort over the past two decades for a variety of important projects, including innovative, low-cost housing in Venice and Santa Monica; the first single-room occupancy hotel to be built on "Skid Row" in Los Angeles in thirty years; offices for film production companies; a municipal gymnasium; and additions to the historic Los Angeles Farmer's Market. Her belief that design excellence can be achieved despite a restricted budget, and her commitment to socially significant projects, have been driving forces in the firm, and the national and international success of the projects has helped refocus attention on those issues.

Selected Awards

Savings by Design Energy Efficiency Integration Award, for 25th Street Studio, 2000

Westside Urban Forum Prize, for the Avalon Hotel, 2000

American Institute of Architects (AIA) California Council Honor Award, for PS #1 Elementary School, 2000

AIA California Council Merit Award, for 5th Street Affordable Family Housing, 2000

AIA Los Angeles Chapter Merit Award, for 5th Street Affordable Family Housing, 1999

City of Santa Monica Sustainable Design Award, for PS #1 Elementary School, 1999

Los Angeles Urban Beautification Award, for Signal Hill Golf Center, 1999

AIA California Council Honor Award, for Tarzana House, 1998

AIA Los Angeles Chapter Merit Award, for PS #1 Elementary School, 1999

AIA Los Angeles Chapter Merit Award, for 5th Street Affordable Family Housing, 1998

Selected Publications

Cohen, Edie. "Thoroughly Modern." *Interior Design*, January 2000.

Crawford, Margaret. "Los Angeles Dingbat." *Architecture Australia*, May 2000.

Pearson, Clifford. "Avalon Hotel." *Architectural Record*, February 2000.

Slessor, Catherine. "Social Services." *Architectural Review*, November 1999.

Friedman, D. S. "Partners Who Sleep Together: a Lunchtime Conversation." *Practice*, May/June 1997.

Koning Eizenberg: Buildings and Projects. New York: Rizzoli, 1996.

FIRM PROFILE

Koning Eizenberg, a Santa Monica-based architecture and planning firm, is known for its imaginative, site-specific, and people-oriented design approach. The firm's diverse client base includes hospitals, universities, elementary schools, hotels, private companies, and local government agencies.

By using suggestion rather than statement, Koning Eisenberg's buildings encourage visitors to discover space and architecture for themselves, guided by compositional cues, landscape strategies, spacial sequence, and scale change. The result is innovative architecture with a rare kind of humanism. The firm is often selected to develop projects that require creative thinking to tackle complex issues of programming and site use, and has achieved recognition for its groundbreaking work in affordable housing and community-based projects. Its completed work has received numerous awards and has been featured in both professional journals and the mainstream press.

Koning Eizenberg's ongoing interest in landscape has influenced such award-winning designs as the Tarzana House, Sepulveda Gym, and Signal Hill Golf Range. Each design started with the crafting of outside space and used the building as a framework to heighten awareness of light, air, and natural beauty. As with most of their projects, these three required innovative solutions to problems and the coordination of a myriad of agency and community needs.

Selected Clients

A.F. Gilmore Company

CIM Group

Edgemar Development

Ian Schrager Hotels

Los Angeles Community Redevelopment Agency; Department of Recreation and Parks; Unified School District

Santa Monica Department of Community and Economic Development; Community Corporation

Skid Row Housing Trust

St. Johns Hospital and Health Center

University of California, Los Angeles; Santa Barbara

DESIGN STATEMENT

Design is exhilarating, and the challenges inherent in the design process are stimulating—getting an idea out, working with people, reconciling program and concept intent, eliciting responses, flushing out ideas, and so on.

Also challenging, but less satisfying, is persevering through the bureaucratic, financial, and implementation aspects of architecture. In the end, it is all worth it.

ILLUSTRATED PROJECTS

Signal Hill Golf Center Driving Range, Santa Monica, California, 1998: A strong graphic approach and energetic, unconventional forms play off a gritty site being transformed from industrial use to a more diversified commercial base.

Felsen Jewelry, Bergamot Station, Santa Monica, California, 1998: A simple contemporary aesthetic matches the jewelry showcased within. Materials were chosen for their evocativeness and to meet the tight budget.

Rare Medium, Los Angeles, California, 1998: In an existing warehouse interior, this office for an expanding multi-media firm was an exercise in spatial sequence, texture, light, and the art of the "easy" detail.

5th Street Family Housing, Santa Monica, California, 1998: Units of affordable housing are organized around a common space with play equipment and a walk street to foster neighborliness. The majority of residents have access to private yards.

Boyd Hotel, Los Angeles, California, 1996: This hotel on "Skid Row" draws on the city's tradition of 1930s architecture, with a welcoming facade, simple yet articulated side elevations, an exterior courtyard, and common areas for interaction.

[Below] **Signal Hill Golf Center Driving Range, Santa Monica, California:**
1&2 Exterior. Photo credit: Grant Mudford

[Above] **Felsen Jewelry, Bergamot Station, Santa Monica, California:** Interior view.
Photo credit: Grant Mudford

[Below] **5th Street Family Housing, Santa Monica, California:** 1 Exterior; 2 Internal courtyard. Photo credit: Grant Mudford

[Above] **Boyd Hotel, Los Angeles, California:** 1 Exterior detail; 2 Entrance hall. Photo credit: Benny Chan

[Left] **Rare Medium, Los Angeles, California:** 1&2 Interior views. Photo credit: Benny Chan

Merrill Elam
United States of America

"The search for broader meanings and possibilities is the phenomenon of architecture that continues to fascinate us."

PROFESSIONAL HISTORY

Merrill Elam received a bachelor of arts in architecture at the Georgia Institute of Technology in 1971 and a master's in business administration at Georgia State University in 1983.

In 1984, Elam, together with Mack Scogin, Ennis Parker, and Lloyd Bray, founded Parker and Scogin Architects in Atlanta, Georgia. In 1986 the firm was reconfigured as Scogin Elam and Bray Architects, Inc., and then in 2000 became Mack Scogin Merrill Elam Architects, Inc.

Elam's work has received national and regional awards and international recognition. She has served as an adjudicator for academic and professional organizations and has lectured and taught at universities throughout the United States. In 1994, she held the Louis Henri Sullivan Chair in Architecture at the University of Illinois in Chicago. In the 1991–1992 academic year, she was the Harry S. Shure Professor at the University of Virginia and the William Wayne Caudill Visiting Lecturer at Rice University.

Elam is a corporate member of the American Institute of Architects (AIA), a founding member and past president of the Architecture Society of Atlanta, past president and member of the Georgia State Board of Architects, and a past member of the board of directors of Art Papers.

Selected Awards

South Atlantic Region AIA Honor Award, 2000, 1994, 1992, 1988, 1987, 1979

Georgia AIA Design Award, 1999, 1997

National AIA Honor Award for Excellence, 1999, 1993, 1992, 1991, 1987

Architectural Record Houses Award, 1998, 1997, 1991

Architectural Record Interiors Award, 1996

Chrysler Award for Innovation, Chrysler Corporation, 1996

Academy Award in Architecture, American Academy of Arts and Letters, 1995

Georgia AIA Award for Excellence in Architecture, 1993, 1990

Silver Medal for Consistent Pursuit and Achievement in Architectural Design, Atlanta Chapter of the AIA, 1989

Honored for Achievement in Architecture at the celebration of "Women's Work," sponsored by Atlanta Women in Film, 1983

Competition Winner, for "A Tower of the Southern Memories," Arts Festival of Atlanta, 1982

Selected Publications

Young, Jason. "Mack and Merrill: The 1999 Charles and Ray Eames Lecture." *Michigan Architecture Press*, 1999.

Andersen, Kurt. "Clayton County Headquarters Library." *Time*, January 1998.

Giovannini, Joseph. "Maine Frame." *Architecture*, March 1998.

Iovine, Julie. "Return to Innovation in a House that Dares." *The New York Times*, 2 July 1998.

Stein, Karen. "Record Houses: 64 Wakefield Drive, Atlanta." *Architectural Record*, April 1998.

Welch, John. "Desert Storm." *RIBA Journal*, January 1998.

Elam, Merrill. "John J. Ross-William C. Blakley Law Library." *Architecture + Urbanism*, March 1995.

FIRM PROFILE

Mack Scogin Merrill Elam Architects, Inc. is organized around the complementary skills of the two principals, Mack Scogin and Merrill Elam, both of whom participate in all projects on a daily basis. They have extensive experience in the formation and leadership of multidisciplined project teams, and bring the understanding of large projects and organizations to a personal practice in architecture.

All staff members are architects or intern architects and collaborate fully on the work. Projects realized by the firm are diverse in size, type, and location. In addition to architecture, services offered by the firm include graphic design, exhibit design, and interior design, planning, and programming.

Prior to founding Mack Scogin Merrill Elam, the principals worked with a third principal, Lloyd Bray, as part of Scogin Elam and Bray Architects, also based in Atlanta. The three worked together for more than twenty-five years, starting with tenures at Heery and Heery Architects in Atlanta, a large, multidisciplinary architectural and construction management firm. While executing design and management work for project types ranging from airports and hospitals to corporate and industrial complexes, Elam and Scogin gained extensive experience in the techniques of controlling the time, cost, and project delivery processes for multifaceted, demanding projects. It is this experience, combined with an unyielding commitment to meeting the needs of clients with inventive architecture, which most distinguishes the firm's work.

Clients of Mack Scogin Merrill Elam expect innovative design with a mature approach to the practical constraints of architecture. The firm's involvement in architecture goes beyond mere problem solving to questions that address architecture's larger role in today's society.

Project types range from educational institutions, public libraries, and arts facilities, to corporate and residential structures. Current and recent work includes the Rheingold Residence in Brookline, Massachusetts; the Knowlton School of Architecture at Ohio State University in Columbus, Ohio; Herman Miller Georgia Operations Consolidation in Cherokee County, Georgia; and the Lee B. Philmon Branch Library in Riverdale, Georgia.

Selected Clients

Arizona State University Board of Regents

Atlanta-Fulton Public Library System

The City of Atlanta/CODA

Clayton County Library Board of Trustees

Corning Enterprises, Inc.

Don and Sylvia Shaw Salon and Spa

Georgia-Pacific Corporation

Herman-Miller, Inc.

The Ohio State University

Tulane University

Turner Broadcasting System, Inc.

University of California, Berkeley

DESIGN STATEMENT

"The Design Challenge"

Although individual design challenges are bound up in and met during the making of discrete projects, "the design challenge," as a general concept, belongs to the greater project, which is architecture itself. Architecture questions what and why, how, and to what end, but in terms that transcend specific projects. The fact that the answers to questions arising from the most recently completed constructions are never completely satisfactory or adequate attests to the ever-present, insistent challenge of the project of architecture.

ILLUSTRATED PROJECTS

John J. Ross-William C. Blakley Law Library, Arizona State University, Tempe, Arizona, 1993

Carol Cobb Turner Branch Library, Morrow, Georgia, 1991

Nomentana Residence, Lovell, Maine, 1997

Don and Sylvia Shaw Salon and Spa, Atlanta, Georgia, 1995

64 Wakefield, Atlanta, Georgia, ongoing

John J. Ross-William C. Blakley Law Library, Arizona State University, Tempe, Arizona: 1 East elevation, showing the dynamic forms of the new law library, located on the fringe of the orthogonally planned campus; 2 An "oasis-like" plaza links the existing law school and the new library, creating a law campus within the greater university campus; 3 Interior view of circulation desk and entry area. Forms and spaces are organized over and around distinct functions. Exterior and interior work in concert to modulate the intense Arizona sun, providing myriad architectural experiences. Photo credit: Timothy Hursley

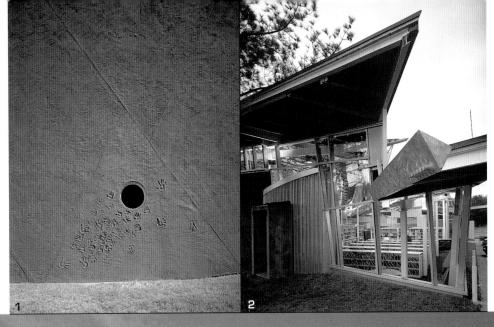

Carol Cobb Turner Branch Library, Morrow, Georgia: 1 Detail with children's handprints. Exterior walls are of glass and Georgia red clay-colored synthetic stucco; 2 Detail at children's area. Just outside is a small garden and reflecting ditch; 3 East elevation. The asymmetrical plan has a dividing breezeway/corridor with rooms off both sides, skewed up toward the bright blue sky and away from the flat, heat-filled, hostile site. Connections to other community buildings and neighborhoods, the points of the compass, and property lines all give form to the building. A vertical steel and glass tower serves as a negative center support, from which the mushroom-like roof emerges on a simple post-and-beam structure. Photo credit: Timothy Hursley

Nomentana Residence, Lovell, Maine: 1 Western elevation, showing forms added onto forms. Rooms are always in spatial and visual continuation, giving the impression of small "house-towns" that resist feelings of isolation in the rural Maine setting; 2 View from living room deck toward pond and mountains; 3 View of living room toward deck; 4 View of entry/library. Photo credit: Timothy Hursley

[Below] **Don and Sylvia Shaw Salon Spa, Atlanta, Georgia:** 1 View of entry. The atmosphere is clean and sparkly but quiet and private, allowing each client to be moved from pleasure to pleasure while feeling the sole occupant of the spa; 2 Detail of stairwell that separates upper level of manicures and pedicures from lower level of more extended services. Photo credit: Timothy Hursley

[Above] **64 Wakefield, Atlanta, Georgia:** 1 Westward view of lap pool and bedroom. Only the 70-foot width of the site was long enough for the pool, so it was installed on the second floor, shielded from the street by a translucent glass wall but open to sky and air; 2 South elevation, showing wood frame structure with stucco and glass enclosing surfaces; 3 View from bedroom stair. Interior materials include painted gypsum wall board and cementitions. Photo credit: Timothy Hursley

Merrill Elam 59

Karen Fairbanks
United States of America

"Rather than formalizing specific spatial and programmatic relationships, our design methodologies focus on architecture as a strategy to establish conditions for these relationships to occur. Much of our work deals with organizations that encourage multiple patterns and combinations of use."

PROFESSIONAL HISTORY

Karen Fairbanks received received a bachelor of science in architecture from the University of Michigan in 1981. From 1981 to 1984 she practiced with Graham Gund Associates, and in 1987 received a master's in architecture from Columbia University. From 1987 to 1989 Fairbanks practiced with Cooper, Robertson & Partners. In 1986 she was the representative for Columbia University in the SOM Traveling Scholarship Competition. Others awards include the Fred L. Liebman Book Award, New York Society of Architects (1986); William Kinne Fellowship for "Japanese Theatral Space: Body, Movement, Form" (1987); an American Institute of Architects (AIA) Medal, Columbia University (1987); a Creative Time Grant (1988); and a New York Foundation for the Arts Fellowship in Architecture (1988). Fairbanks has also served as a panelist for the Architecture Awards for the New York Foundation for the Arts and on the Young Architects Committee for the Architectural League of New York. In 1990 Fairbanks and Scott Marble co-founded Marble • Fairbanks Architects in New York City.

Academic appointments include: visiting critic for the Parsons School of Design in 1991 and Rensselaer Polytechnic Institute in 1993, adjunct assistant professor of architecture at Columbia University from 1988–1996, director of the Program in Architecture for Columbia College from 1991 to the present, and senior lecturer in architecture and director of the Program in Architecture for Barnard and Columbia Colleges from 1996 to the present.

Selected Awards: Marble • Fairbanks

AIA Design Award, 1999, 1997, 1996, 1994

Emerging Architecture and Design Award, *The Architectural Review* and d line, 1999

Emerging Voices, Architectural League of New York, 1998

40 Under 40, New York, 1996

New York Foundation for the Arts Fellowship in Architecture, 1994

Architectural League of New York Young Artists Forum, Urban Center (work selected for exhibition), 1992

Finalist (one of 5 from more than 600 entries), NARA Convention Hall International Design Competition, Nara, Japan, 1991

Selected Publications

Bussel, Abby. "The Learning Curve." *Interior Design*, May 2000.

Davey, Peter. "Emerging Architecture" and "Just the Ticket." *The Architectural Review*, December 1999.

Rus, Mayer. *Loft*. New York: The Monacelli Press, 1998.

Cunningham, Michael. "Guiding Light: New Materials Open Spaces." *Metropolitan Home*, March/April 1997.

Kansai-kan of the National Diet Library. *AIA Annals*, 1996–1997.

"Take Four; Alternative Designs for the Cardiff Bay Opera House." *World Architecture*, January 1996.

"First Stage Winner: Scott Marble and Karen Fairbanks." [Special feature on Nara Convention Hall International Design Competition.] *The Japan Architect*, Summer 1992–1993.

FIRM PROFILE

Scott Marble and Karen Fairbanks of Marble • Fairbanks Architects began collaborating in 1990; prior to 1990, they were principals in separate practices and completed several small- and large-scale projects in and around New York City. They have taught at Columbia University since 1988, investigating themes and issues present in their built work.

Over the past decade the firm has worked on a wide range of residential, commercial, and institutional projects, providing complete architectural services from schematic design through construction. All of the firm's projects are developed by both partners with a project architect and the Marble • Fairbanks staff, and the studio team follows the project from preliminary planning to completion.

Selected Clients

Columbia University, *New York City*

The Cooper Union for the Advancement of Science and Art, *New York City*

Museum of Modern Art, *New York City*

Our Children's Foundation, *New York City*

DESIGN STATEMENT

Although different projects facilitate different degrees of conceptual investigation, we understand all of our work in a social and cultural context that conditions the specifics of each project.

We have most recently been investigating the potential of architecture to embrace both the space of a global network and the more specific space of a given site, program(s), and time. While acknowledging the emergence of a linked world culture, we work with the premise that societies and cultures at the turn of the millennium are still heterogeneous entities with instances of unique and distinctive characteristics, which architecture can and should embody. To attempt to erase these distinctions limits the possibility of revealing the most potent and active critical tendencies of society—those existing and already within.

Interpretations and elaborations of the cultural and programmatic, as well as physical, context surrounding an architectural project play instrumental roles in how we conceive of our work. Consequently, we have begun to think about architecture as *intervention* that absorbs and reconfigures, rather than confronts, context. Much of our work deals with spatial organizations that encourage multiple patterns of use, acknowledging the constructive dynamic between the context and the architectural intervention. Rather than formalizing specific spatial and programmatic relationships, our design methodology focuses on architecture as a strategy to establish *conditions for these relationships to occur*. The architectural intervention reframes the existing context and potentially reprograms public use, provoking new forms of social exchange.

ILLUSTRATED PROJECTS

The Louis and Jeanette Brooks Engineering Design Center, The Cooper Union, New York City, 1998

Cardiff Opera House, Cardiff, Wales, 1994

Kansai-Kan of the National Diet Library, Kansai, Japan, 1996

Seibert Residence, New York City, 1994

NARA Convention Hall, Nara, Japan, 1992

Chelsea Loft, New York City, 1994

The Louis and Jeannette Brooks Engineering Design Center, the Cooper Union, New York City: 1 Reflected ceiling plan; 2 View from multimedia classroom into computer lab. Sliding doors and curtains allow flexibility for the center's changing needs; 3 View from computer lab into multimedia classroom. Individuals can work alone at workstations, groups can gather at tables, and large groups can meet in multimedia classroom; 4 Glass wall between the classroom and hallway becomes an interactive zone where student movement, objects produced, and exhibitions are all displayed. Photo credit: Eduard Hueber

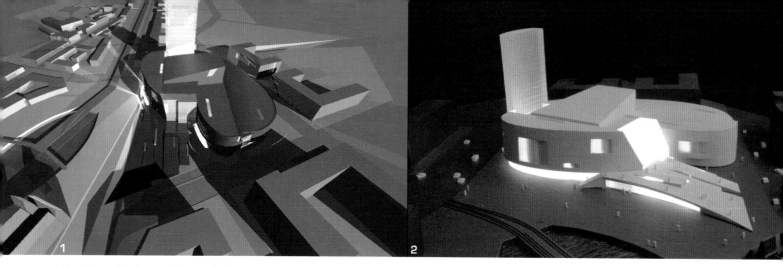

[Above] **Cardiff Opera House, Cardiff, Wales:** 1 Computer rendering of aerial view. The building's site, at a juncture between two roads and a harbor, has formal and programmatic conditions that have been absorbed into the building; 2 The building envelope begins internally (the proscenium of the theater) and emerges as an exterior wrapper moving around the site and ending at the sloping entry ramps. Photo credits: courtesy Marble • Fairbanks Architects [1]; Eduard Hueber [2]

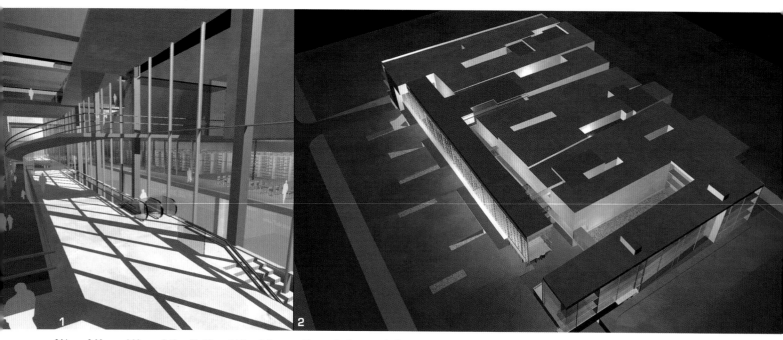

[Above] **Kansai-Kan of the National Diet Library, Kansai, Japan:** 1 Computer rendering of "information exchange," a crossroads in the library that encourages both physical and electronic exchanges of information; 2 Aerial perspective, showing reading rooms spread throughout the stacks. Photo credit: courtesy Marble • Fairbanks Architects

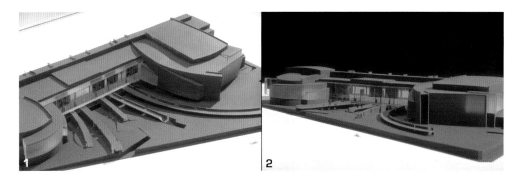

[Left] **NARA Convention Hall, Nara, Japan:** 1&2 Models. Both the physical structure and activities within this theater are used to create context for the site. A procenium strip with electronic screens and an interior walkway runs the length of the site, conecting the two main halls and organizing both the building and the plaza. Photo credit: Eduard Hueber

[Above] **Chelsea Loft, New York City:** 1 Pivoting doors into bedroom. The doors are parallelograms that pivot asymetrically; 2 A lowered ceiling articulates the relationship between the breakfast room and the kitchen within the loft's open space; 3 View across living spaces, showing four sliding wood and glass panels and three pivoting doors that divide the space; 4 The bedroom, showing negotiation of degrees of privacy within open loft. Photo credit: Peter Paige

[Left] **Siebert Residence, New York City:** 1 Space is organized through a series of dynamic planes which modulate relationships between adjacent spaces, such as this glass and acrylic rod wall between the living room and bedroom; 2 Living room, showing cherry flooring that extends under the planes to connect adjacent spaces. Photo credit: Paul Warchol

Zaha Hadid
United Kingdom

*"I believe architects, like artists, have the possibility of making culture.
Like artists, architects should strive to be slightly ahead of everybody else,
so they can focus attention on what's happening."*

PROFESSIONAL HISTORY AND FIRM PROFILE

Zaha Hadid is a London-based architectural designer whose work encompasses all fields of design, ranging from the urban scale to products, interiors, and furniture. Central to her concerns is a simultaneous engagement in practice, teaching, and research, in the pursuit of an uncompromising commitment to modernism.

Hadid studied architecture at the Architectural Association (AA) and was awarded the Diploma Prize in 1977. She then became a partner of the Office for Metropolitan Architecture (OMA), began teaching at the AA with OMA collaborators Rem Koolhaas and Elia Zenghelis, and later led her own studio at the AA until 1987. Since then she has held the Kenzo Tange Chair at Harvard University's Graduate School of Design, the Sullivan Chair at the University of Chicago School of Architecture, and guest professorships at the Hochschule für Bildende Künste in Hamburg, the Knolton School of Architecture in Ohio, and the Master's Studio at Columbia University. She is the current Eero Saarinen Visiting Professor of Architectural Design at Yale University in New Haven. In addition, she is an honorary member of the American Academy of Arts and Letters and a fellow of the American Institute of Architecture (AIA).

Hadid has tested the boundaries of architectural design in a series of competitions. Winning designs include the Cardiff Bay Opera House, Wales (1994); the Contemporary Arts Center, Cincinnati (1998); University of North London Holloway Road Bridge (1998); the Center for Contemporary Arts, Rome (1999); and the Bergisi ski jump in Innsbruck, Austria (1999).

Hadid's built work has won her much academic and public acclaim. Her best known projects to date are the Vitra Fire Station and the LF One pavilion in Weil am Rhein, Germany (1993 and 1999, see pages 68 and 69); a housing project for IBA-Block 2, Berlin (1993); and the Mind Zone at the Millennium Dome in Greenwich, London (1999, see page 68). She has also completed furniture and interiors, exhibition designs, installations, and stage sets.

Hadid's paintings and drawings have always been an important testing field and a medium for the exploration of her design, and have been widely published in periodicals and monographs (see Selected Publications). She has had major exhibitions at the Guggenheim Museum, New York City (1978); the AA,

London (1983); the GA Gallery, Tokyo (1985); the Museum of Modern Art (MoMA), New York (1988); Harvard University's Graduate School of Design (1995); Grand Central Station, New York (1995); and MoMA San Francisco (1997–1998). Her work is also in the permanent collections of various institutions, including MoMA New York, MoMA San Francisco, and the Deutsches Architektur Museum in Frankfurt.

Current commissions include contemporary arts centers for Cincinnati and Rome (see page 69); a ski jump in Innsbruck, Austria; a breeding center for endangered species in Qatar; a major bridge structure in Abu Dhabi, UAE; a landscape design for the Strasbourg Tramway; a science center in Wolfsburg, Germany; and a ferry terminal in Salerno, Italy.

Selected Publications

Hadid, Zaha with M. Schumacher et al. *LF One: Landscape Formation One in Weil am Rhein, Germany*. Boston: Birkhauser, 1999.

Interview with Zaha Hadid on Contemporary Arts Center, Cincinnati, posted on the Internet at www.spiral. org/newbuildings6.html, 1999

Hadid, Zaha and Aaron Betsky. *Zaha Hadid: The Complete Buildings and Projects*. New York: Rizzoli, 1998.

Taylor, David. "Zaha's Daring Mind Zone Designs Unveiled." *Architects' Journal*, 26 November 1998.

Crickhowell, Nicholas. *Opera House Lottery: Zaha Hadid and the Cardiff Bay Project*. University of Wales Press, 1997

Selected Clients

Cities of Weil am Rhein and Wolfsburg, *Germany*
Cincinnati Contemporary Arts Center
University of North London
Abu Dhabi Public Works Department
Center for Contemporary Art, *Rome*
Pet Shop Boys
Town Council of Salerno, *Italy*
Vitra International

DESIGN STATEMENT

Mind Zone, Millennium Dome, Greenwich, UK

The Mind Zone is one of fourteen exhibition spaces within the Millennium Dome. The design engages the complex subject matter of the mind in a structure of three overlapping sections, which unfold to create a continuous surface that can serve as floor, wall, or ceiling, providing for a fluid journey through the space.

The content of the exhibit and the exhibit surface are presented and experienced as a single idea; the exhibit structure of folding continuous surfaces is seen as a host, the physical presence on which, and within which, the exhibit's content is located.

As a narrative strategy, the three elements—wall, floor, ceiling—complement the primary mental functions—input, process, output—with the continuous flow of the structural elements paralleling the continuous flow of our mental processes. The mental processes are represented variously through perspectival and visual distortion, explanatory exhibits, sculpture, audiovisual installations, and interactive elements.

Because the underlying design strategy was to avoid being overtly pedagogical and to emphasize interactive, thought-provoking elements, it was proposed (and agreed) that artists be the main exhibitors. The exhibit is organized around the artists' installations, leading participants through the exhibit by conditional stages: from the question of what constitutes intelligence to perceptual inputs, through the mechanisms of thought to speculations on cultural and individual malleability.

Structurally, the exhibit integrates its content with the use of new construction materials—those that are still in development and not yet fully established. The exhibit's physical elements are synthetic, created from the mind-made materials of the present.

The brief to create a continuous floor/wall/ceiling has produced a unique, lightweight, transparent panel made of glass fiber "skins" and with an aluminum honeycomb structure. Similarly, the base structure, made of steel, is layered with translucent materials, which create an ephemeral, temporal quality befitting an exhibition whose design life was only one year.

ILLUSTRATED PROJECTS

Mind Zone, Millennium Dome, Greenwich, London, 1999
Landesgartenschau (LF One), Weil am Rhein, Germany, 1999–present
The Center for Contemporary Arts, Rome, Italy, 1999–present
Contemporary Arts Center, Cincinnati, Ohio, 1998–present
Vitra Fire Station, Vitra, Germany, 1993–present

[Below] **Mind Zone, Millennium Done, Greenwich, UK:** 1 Model showing view of main projection space and exit; 2 Model showing view of entrance; 3 View of main canopy with light installation by artists Langlands & Bell. Photo credits: courtesy office of Zaha Hadid [1, 2]; Hélène Binet [3]

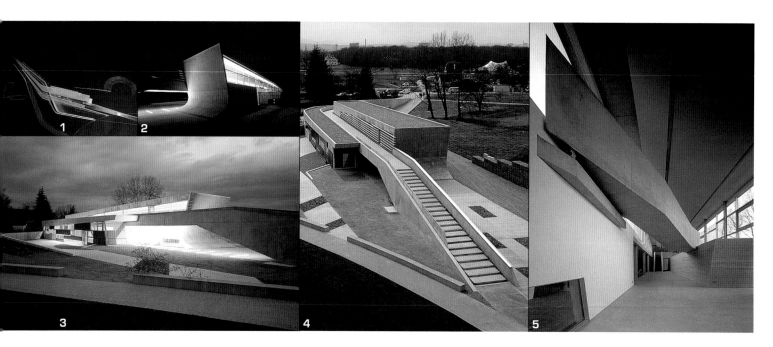

[Above] **Landesgartenschau (LF One), Weil am Rhein, Germany:** 1 Exhibition building for landscape and gardening show is itself conceived in terms of landscape features rather than geometric order; 2 View at night; 3 The main facade. The smooth, concrete structure emerges from the fluid geometry of a surrounding network of paths, three of which entangle to make the building; 4 Aerial view of complex, showing one of the paths. The building's geometry extends into the surroundings, inventing artificial landscapes and landforms; 5 Interior view. The main spaces, exhibition hall, and café stretch along the paths for plenty of sunlight and exterior views. Photo credits: Chistian Richters [1, 2, 5]; Hélène Binet [3, 4]

[Below] **The Center for Contemporary Arts, Rome, Italy:** 1 Computer-generated aerial view of arts center; 2 Computer image of urban context; 3 Computer image of exhibition spaces. Photo credit: courtesy office of Zaha Hadid

[Above] **Contemporary Art Center, Cincinnati, Ohio:** 1–3 Computer images of new arts center for temporary exhibitions. As visitors enter, the ground level curves slowly upward to become the back wall of the center, called the "Urban Carpet"—an element that mediates between city, lobby, and galleries beyond. As it rises and turns, the Urban Carpet leads visitors up a suspended mezzanine ramp through the lobby, conceived as a free public space. Ramps rise and fall in this "free zone," creating a series of highly polished, undulating surfaces that contrast with rawer concrete galleries above. Photo credit: courtesy office of Zaha Hadid

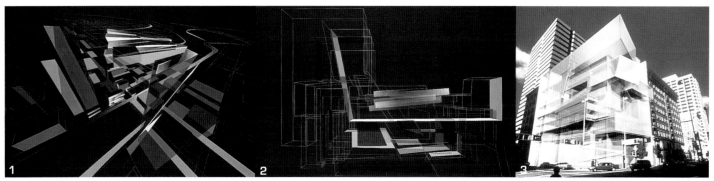

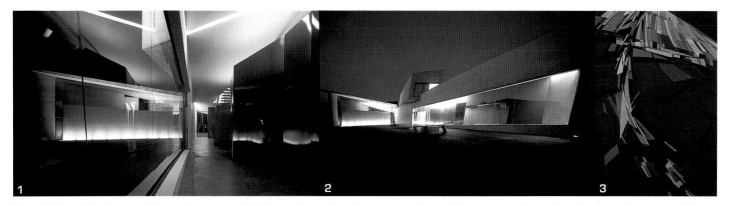

[Above] **Vitra Fire Station, Vitra, Germany:** 1–3 Linear, layered walls puncture, tilt, and break according to functional requirements of the fire station. Movement is inscribed into the building: that of the fire engines as well as of the ritualized exercises of the firemen. The design is movement frozen, expressing the tension of being on constant alert. Lines of light allow for fast, precise movement throughout the building. Photo credits: Paul Warchol [1, 2], courtesy office of Zaha Hadid (3)

Frances Halsband
United States of America

*"Our work is the creation of places that engage
the past and give form to the future."*

PROFESSIONAL HISTORY

Frances Halsband was born in New York City. She received her bachelor of arts from Swarthmore College in 1965, and a master's in architecture from Columbia University in 1968. After traveling and studying in Europe on a William Kinne Fellowship, she returned to New York to work in the office of Mitchell/Giurgola. In 1972, she co-founded R. M. Kliment & Frances Halsband Architects with Robert Kliment.

Halsband has taught at the universities of Ball State, California at Berkeley, Columbia, Harvard, North Carolina State, Pennsylvania, Rice, and Virginia. She has served on numerous design award juries and was the 1999 chair of the Committee on Design for the American Institute of Architects (AIA).

From 1991 to 1994, Halsband was dean of the School of Architecture at the Pratt Institute. She has been a team member of the National Architectural Accrediting Board and a regional director of the Association of Collegiate Schools of Architecture. She is publisher of the Design History Foundation journal *Places*.

Halsband has served as president of the New York Chapter of the AIA, president of the Architectural League of New York, and commissioner of the New York Landmarks Preservation Commission. She is currently a member of the architectural review board of the Federal Reserve Bank and the architectural advisory board of the U.S. Department of State Foreign Buildings Operations. She is also a member of the U.S. General Services Administration National Register of Peer Professionals.

Selected Awards: R.M. Kliment & Frances Halsband

AIA New York State Award of Merit, 2000

Interfaith Forum on Religion, Art, and Architecture Design Award, 2000

Chicago Athenaeum American Architecture Award, 1999

General Services Administration Design Award Citation, 1999

AIA New York Chapter Medal of Honor, 1998

AIA Architecture Firm Award, 1997

AIA Honor Award for Excellence in Architectural Design, 1996, 1994, 1987

AIA New York Chapter Excellence in Architecture Award, 1996, 1987, 1985, 1981, 1979, 1978

AIA New York State Award of Excellence, 1996, 1988, 1985, 1982

City Club of New York Bard Award for Excellence in Architecture and Urban Design, 1996, 1989

Cleveland Engineering Society Award of Excellence, 1996

Design for Transportation Award, National Endowment for the Arts, 1996

AIA Honor Award for Excellence in Interior Design, 1994

Cleveland AIA Award for Excellence in Historic Preservation and Restoration, 1994

Cleveland Restoration Society Award of Excellence, 1994

Selected Publications

Dobney, Stephen, ed. *R. M. Kliment & Frances Halsband Architects: Selected and Current Works*. Mulgrave, Australia: The Images Publishing Group, 1998.

Halsband, Frances. "On Partners," in *Equal Partners: Men and Women Principals in Contemporary Architectural Practice*. Northampton, Massachusetts: Smith College Museum of Art, 1998; pp. 48–52.

"R. M. Kliment & Frances Halsband." *Architecture and Urbanism*, January 1996: pp. 94–101.

Halsband, Frances. "Defining Four Streams of Current Thought," *in American Architecture of the 1980s*. Washington, D.C.: American Institute of Architects Press, 1990; pp. 337–338.

Norberg-Schulz, Christian. "The Third Step: The Work of R. M. Kliment & Frances Halsband Architects." *Architecture and Urbanism*, May 1988; pp. 11–54.

FIRM PROFILE

The work of R. M. Kliment & Frances Halsband Architects, a partnership founded in New York City in 1972, includes master planning; buildings for educational, cultural, and corporate clients; civic buildings; residences; additions, renovations, historic preservation, and adaptive reuse; interiors; and furniture and lighting. All of the firm's work is a collaboration of the two founding partners.

R. M. Kliment and Frances Halsband have designed projects as small as an 80-square-foot protoype newsstand and as large as a 2.5-million-square-foot college master plan. Recent commissions include a U.S. courthouse in Gulfport, Mississippi; the Franklin D. Roosevelt Presidential Library Visitors Center in Hyde Park, New York; and the Smith College campus plan in Northampton, Massachusetts.

Selected Clients

Banque Nationale de Paris
College of Wooster
Columbia University
Dartmouth College
Metropolitan Transportation Authority
New York Public Library
New York University
North Carolina Museum of Art
Princeton University
Rockefeller Properties, Inc.
University of Virginia
U.S. General Services Administration
Woodstock Artists' Association
Yale University

DESIGN STATEMENT

We intend our buildings to be clearly conceived and carefully made places that engage the past and imply connections to the future.

We believe it important that our buildings:

- engage the existing cultural and physical context so as to become integral components of it;
- give direction to future uses and development so that change and growth can be natural and coherent;
- fully develop the requirements and opportunities of program, so that they work well; and
- have construction that is congruent with available skills and funds, so that they are built well.

We search for a consistency and clarity of formal expression that is a language of forms, and for materials and details that are expressive of the function and of the spirit of the program and of the site. The result is a language that is matched to building craft, a match of means to an end. Each project varies in relation to its cultural and physical context, and we strive to make each coherent within itself and consistent with the essential intent of our work.

ILLUSTRATED PROJECTS

Columbia University Lamont Doherty Earth Observatory Master Plan, Palisades, New York, 1996

Roth Center for Jewish Life, Dartmouth College, Hanover, New Hampshire, 1997

International Business Technology Management Office, Stamford, Connecticut, 1998

Long Island Railroad Entrance Pavilion to Pennsylvania Station, New York City, 1994

[Below] **Roth Center for Jewish Life, Dartmouth College, Hanover, New Hampshire:** 1 View of the sanctuary facing the ark. The room is lit from above; 2 View of the library from the lower level; 3 View from the southeast shows the campus entrance next to the library, the gallery windows, and the sanctuary beyond; 4 Plans. Photo credits: Peter Aaron/ ESTO [1, 3]; Cervin Robinson [2]

Columbia University Lamont Doherty Earth Observatory Master Plan, Palisades, New York: 1 The historic Hudson River setting (shown here from the north) incorporates new earth sciences laboratories, which overlook the Palisades; 2 Master plan drawing. Rendering: Frances Halsband

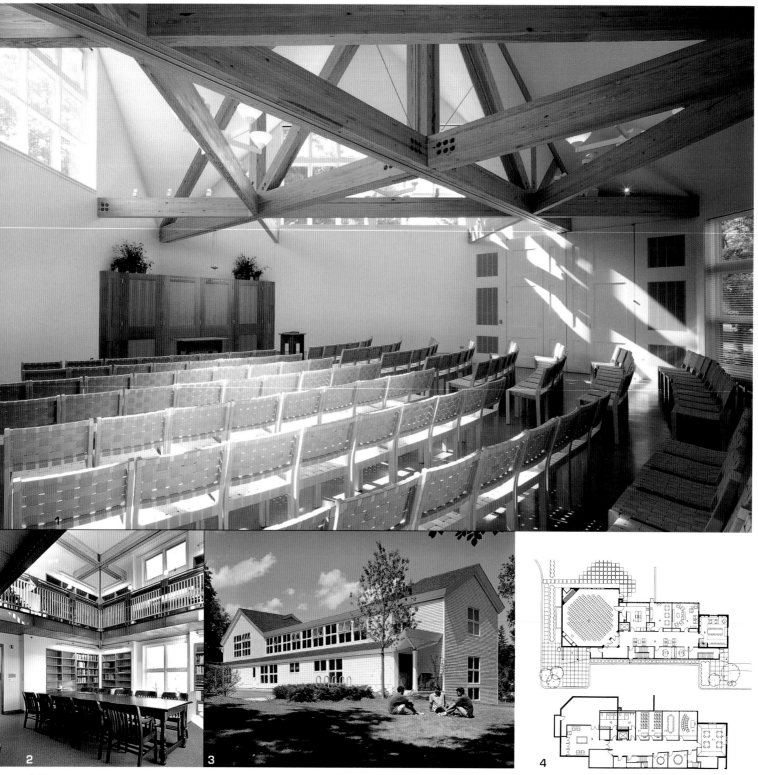

International Business Technology Management Office, Stamford, Connecticut: 1 Floor plan showing piazza at entrance and flexible individual workspaces beyond; 2 The piazza—with its coffee bar, Internet connections, magazine racks, mailboxes, and flat-screen television tuned to business news—encourages informal meetings; 3 Individual consultant workspaces have sliding glass walls for individual activity or communal space. Photo credit: Peter Aaron/ESTO

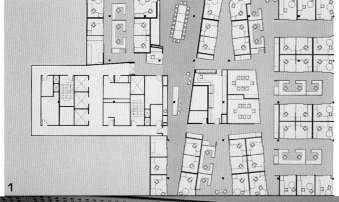

Long Island Railroad Entrance Pavilion to Pennsylvania Station, New York City: 1 New entrance tower (with the Empire State Building in the background) is illuminated by a pendant fixture suspended in space and by uplights set in the four corner columns; 2 Detail of transparent glass tower with suspended clock, which was salvaged from the old Pennsylvania Station. Photo credit: Cervin Robinson

Gisue Hariri & Mojgan Hariri

United States of America

"We believe that in the new millennium the physical form of architecture must change to not only reflect our changing habits and conception of life but to incorporate the new digital technology and telecommunication networks, connecting us globally and allowing us to move between the virtual and actual worlds."

PROFESSIONAL HISTORY

Gisue Hariri graduated from Cornell University with a bachelor's degree in architecture in 1980. Her student projects were exhibited at Philippe Bonnafont Gallery in San Francisco and published in the *Cornell Journal of Architecture*. In 1980 and 1981 she apprenticed at Jennings & Stout Architects in San Francisco; in 1982 she attended construction workshops at Arcosanti, Arizona; and from 1983 to 1985 she practiced as a design architect with Paul Segal Associates Architects.

Since 1987, Gisue Hariri has been an adjunct professor of architecture at Columbia University and has acted as a visiting critic at Cornell University, McGill University, and Parsons School of Design. She has also participated as a jury panel member for awards such as the SOM (Skidmore, Owings & Merrill) Foundation Traveling Fellowship Awards, the American Institute of Architects (AIA) Design Awards, and the I.D. Magazine Annual Design Awards. She has lectured at a variety of institutions and architectural schools, including UCLA, SCI-Arc (Southern California Institute of Architecture), and Syracuse and Rice universities.

Mojgan Hariri received a bachelor's in architecture in 1981 and a master's of architecture in urban design in 1983, both from Cornell University. In 1983, she was awarded the Alexander Eschweiler prize for high scholastic achievement. From 1983 to 1986, she was apprenticed at James Stewart Polshek & Partners in New York City.

In 1986, Gisue Hariri and Mojgan Hariri co-founded Hariri & Hariri in New York City.

Selected Awards

40 Under 40, 1996

Architectural Record Record House, for Barry's Bay Cottage, 1995; for New Canaan House, Connecticut, 1993

Emerging Voices, Architectural League of New York, 1995

I.D. Magazine Award, for JSM Music Studios, 1993

Young Architects Forum, work selected by Architectural League of New York for exhibition at the Urban Center in New York City, 1990

Selected Publications

Richards, Ivor. *Manhattan Lofts*. London: John Wiley & Sons, 2000.

Castle, Helen. "Hariri & Hariri." *Architectural Design*, July-August 1999.

Ojeda, Oscar Riera, ed. *Hariri & Hariri: Essays by Kenneth Frampton and Steven Holl*. New York: The Monacelli Press, 1995; 2nd edition, 1999.

Quici, Fabio. "Hariri & Hariri: moderne abduzioni." *Il Projetto*, July 1999.

Riley, Terence. *The Un-Private House*. New York: Museum of Modern Art, 1999.

Ojeda, Oscar Riera. *Casas International 48: Hariri & Hariri*. Argentina: Kliczkowski, 1997.

Russell, Beverly. *40 Under 40: A Guide to New Young Talent with Seductive Ideas for Living Today*. Grand Rapids, Michigan: Vitae Publ., 1995.

Frampton, Kenneth. "Criticism: On the Work of Hariri & Hariri." *Architecture and Urbanism*, July 1993.

FIRM PROFILE

Gisue and Mojgan Hariri exemplify the spirit of the emerging generation of architects. These gifted sisters, born in Iran and educated at Cornell University, opened Hariri & Hariri in New York City in 1986. Since then, the firm has attracted international attention and its work has been featured in numerous galleries, academic venues, books, and journals. In the August 1988 issue of *House & Garden*, Charles Gandee featured the firm's work, writing "No young New York firm signals the dawn of the new architectural day more emphatically than Hariri & Hariri." In her publication *40 Under 40: A Guide to New Young Talent with Seductive Ideas for Living Today*, Beverly Russell defined the Hariri sisters as "radicals" who "focused on forward-looking technology and materials that define the twenty-first century."

Hariri & Hariri is dedicated to the research and construction of innovative ideas. High style, handicraft, a sense of place, and a social agenda—qualities often considered mutually exclusive—catalytically co-exist in the firm's work. An inventive use of materials and a unique understanding of light and space, together with the principals' philosophical search for the essence of existence, are consistent elements in all of the firm's projects.

The firm's work is organized around a number of important themes—politics and power, global culture, materiality, paradoxical reality, and otherness—all of which have influenced the architects' design and practice. Regarding architecture and contemporary culture,

the Hariris say, "What is important in terms of cultural connections is the spirituality of Eastern thinking, which we are evaluating in the West, or rather from which we are evaluating the Western culture."

Selected Clients

JSM Music Studios, *New York City*

House Beautiful (Digital House)

Geerlings Vastgood, B.V. (design for single-family villa), *The Hague*

George Kovacs (Stasis lighting collection)

Tui Pranich, *Pranich Showroom, Miami*

DESIGN STATEMENT

We do not believe in chaos,

We do not believe in trends, and

We despise kitsch.

It is our intention to grasp and to convey that all events and things perceived by the senses are connected and interrelated, and are different aspects or manifestations of the same reality. For us, architecture is a metaphysical path beyond its physical destination.

ILLUSTRATED PROJECTS

The Digital House, 1998, sponsored by House Beautiful, *MoMA Un-Private House Exhibition, 1999:* This design for a *House Beautiful* project uses active-matrix LCD panels as both a building material and a receiver and transmitter of information.

Riverbend House, Virginia, 1995: One part of the house is earthbound, with a heavy masonry structure that follows the contour of the land; this volume contains the bedrooms and other private spaces. The second part is sky bound, its light, winglike structure supported by steel columns and enclosed mostly by glass curtain walls; the roof is a folded plane that lifts upward as it stretches over the house, emphasizing the human desire for weightlessness. This second volume contains the home's public spaces.

Greenwich House, Greenwich, Connecticut, 1996: A 3,800-square-foot home reexamines suburban living for the new millennium. Separate volumes contain the children's rooms, the living and dining rooms, and the master suite, connected by an open media room. Walls are translucent fiberglass with occasional sections of clear glass, providing filtered light by day and a lantern-like glow on the outside at night.

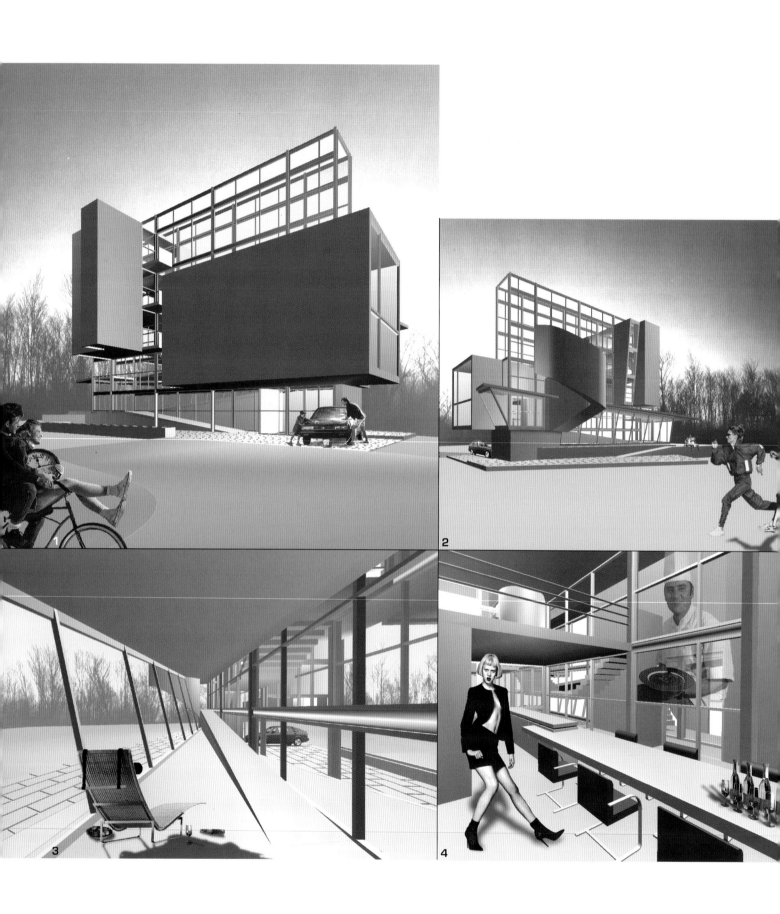

The Digital House: 1 Exterior view. LCD panels allow exterior walls to change color and content according to owner's mood; 2 Driveway, carport, and plugged-in volumes; 3 Entry hall; transient space with ramp; 4 Living and dining room, with LCD panel that can be changed daily, this one reflecting a virtual cooking lesson. Photo credit: courtesy Hariri & Hariri

Riverbend House, Virginia: 1 Exterior view from slope at west; 2 Prow of projection with winglike roof; 3 Entrance hall with the main staircase;
4 Living room with fireplace wall. Photo credit: ESTO Photographics, Inc.

[Opposite and below] **Greenwich House, Greenwich, Connecticut:** 1 Entry at dusk, with translucent fiberglass curtain; 2 Dining room; 3 Living room looking toward media room; 4 Exterior view from north, showing variation of opacity, translucency, and transparency. Photo credit: Jason Schmidt

Jane Harrison
United Kingdom

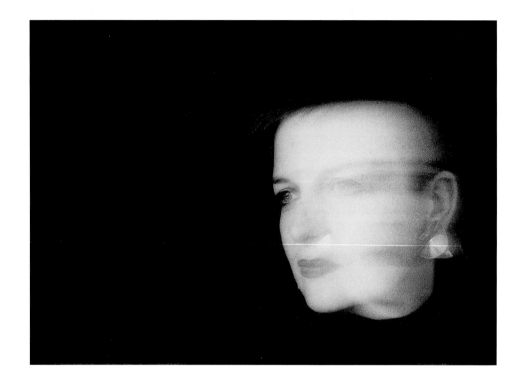

"Architecture now must find ways of producing a condition that intervenes in the media-saturated world without resorting to the mind-numbing dullness of the banal or the instant gratification of the merely spectacular. An architecture founded on a contemporary synthesis of ecology, electronics, and economics can do this."

PROFESSIONAL HISTORY

Jane Harrison was born in London and educated in England, Switzerland, and the United States. She studied music, mathematics, and computer science before taking her initial degree in architecture at Rice University in Houston, Texas and later continuing her studies at the Architectural Association (AA) in London. She worked for Sir Norman Foster in London until 1991, when she began a working partnership with David Turnbull and the two were invited to establish a unit at the AA. In 1995, Harrison and Turnbull co-founded atopos: architecture<>urbanism.

In 1996, Harrison and Turnbull collaborated on a 96-page monograph, *Games of Architecture*, the revolutionary nature of which is clear from the way it is cataloged by the Library of Congress—under the subject headings "Architecture, Modern," "Avant-garde (Aesthetics)," and "Play (Philosophy)." They are currently working on another book, *Fast Cities*, a comprehensive collection of the firm's urban research work over the past five years.

Since leaving the AA in 1996, Harrison has conducted advanced research studios on the potential of numerical algorithms and nonlinear thinking for architecture and urbanism at Yale University, where she has collaborated with structural engineer Cecil Balmond, and at Columbia University. She is currently on the faculty of the Metropolitan Research and Design Program at SCI-Arc in Los Angeles, and was recently appointed to a lifetime professorship at the Vienna University of Technology in Austria.

Selected Exhibitions

Desire, FOE156, Munich, 1999

In the Midst of Things, Bournville, England, 1999

Unquiet Urbanism, White Box, New York City, 1999

City, Space + Globalization, University of Michigan, Ann Arbor, Michigan, 1998

Intimate Space, Stux Gallery, New York City, 1998

Unmapping the Earth: Space/Fire—1997, Kwangju Biennale, Korea, 1997

Selected Publications

A Utopian Manual. London: August Books, 2000.

Jencks, Charles. *Ecstatic Architecture: the Surprising Link*. New York: Academy Editions, 1999.

Harrison, Jane. "Multiplication + Subdivision 1," in *Architecture of Fear*. New York: Princeton Architectural Press, 1997.

"Production and Operativity." *Arhitektov Bilten [Architect's Bulletin]*. July 1997.

"'Roadworks' in Art and Architecture." *Architectural Design*, May/June 1997.

"'Flatscapes' in Anthropology and Architecture." *Architectural Design*, 11 December 1996.

Harrison, Jane and David Turnbull (ed.). "Games of Architecture." *Architectural Design*, May/June 1996.

FIRM PROFILE

Based in both London and New York, atopos is organized according to a network model, which allows it to maximize flexibility and speed of response and facilitate rescaling to suit the demands of each project. The firm has extensive experience in the areas of planning, architecture, landscape design, exhibition design, and design research. Its range of projects includes museums, theaters, and other institutional facilities; commercial buildings; urban infrastructures; and residential works.

One area of expertise is the design of interactive public surfaces. The outdoor surface of the Constantini Museum (see page 83), for example, is wired so that water, sound, and lighting effects shift in response to changes in the surrounding environment, such as fluctuations in traffic flow. The firm specializes in the development of what they call "effects infrastructures," designs that challenge the conventional distinctions between a building and the surrounding public space, producing unique effects and new kinds of environment.

Recent projects include the strategic planning and design of a media studies and theater complex for Brunel University's Uxbridge campus, located near Heathrow Airport (see Boilerhouse Theatre, page 82); work at the Tate Gallery in Liverpool; planning studies for new districts in Leicester and Cheltenham; the restructuring of Walton Heath Golf Club, one of the premier golf clubs in the UK (see page 82); a new urban infrastructure and extension to a Fachhochschule for Graz West in Austria; and a design prototype for marina operations centers for the south coast of England.

Selected Clients

Graz City Planning Department, *Graz, Austria*

Tate Gallery, *Liverpool, England*

James Stirling Foundation, *London*

The Trustees of the Tate Gallery, *London*

Craig Development, *Fairfax County, Virginia*

Elpro AG (atopos with OAP International), *Berlin*

Multi Vastgoed (atopos with OAP International), *The Hague*

DESIGN STATEMENT

The work of atopos occupies the "analytic borderland" between the physical and the virtual.

Our design work is grounded by research that focuses on the operational modalities of the contemporary city, including new patterns of development; distributions of density; new qualities of light, weight, and movement; and heightened psychological states. The algorithms that guide patterns of use and fluctuations in intensity are tracked, as are the physical and social effects of today's vast electronic networks of telecommunication and data transfer. Our work uses these effects; we employ architecture's capacity to alter or enhance the psycho-spatial qualities of contemporary life and deploy abstract "a-dimensional" structures (those involving topological, rather than dimensional, relationships), speculative form, and new composite materials in projects that operate at multiple scales. Every project is specific, avoiding superficial stylistic continuities.

ILLUSTRATED PROJECTS

Multiplication + Subdivision, Forms of Fairfax County, 1996–current

Minimum Global City Installation, Korean Biennale, 1996–current: A 30-by 6-foot billboard with text and images outlining ten new categories for understanding the behavior of contemporary cities.

Boilerhouse Theatre, Brunel University, West London, stage one completed 1998: Former machine rooms of a campus boiler house, now to be used as an experimental theater. The eco-industrial quilted surface made of recycled plastics establishes the building as part of the university's cultural infrastructure.

Walton Heath Golf Club, Surrey, UK, 1997–current

Costantini Museum, Buenos Aires, Argentina, proposed 1998

Hotel Lago Espejo, Argentina, proposed 1999

"Better Living" terrain, Bournville, Birmingham, UK, 1999

[Below] **Multiplication + Subdivision, forms of Fairfax County, Virginia:** Ongoing research into the proliferation of non-hierarchical fields of suburban sprawl—in this case, plan diagrams of roads in the subdivisions of Fairfax County, Virginia. The "grid" of a traditional city has been replaced with these forms, produced through rigorous adherence to the logic of traffic flow.

[Above] **Minimum Global City Billboard Installation, Korean Biennale** Photo credit: courtesy atopos: architecture<>urbanism

[Above] **Boilerhouse Theater, Brunel University, West London** Photo credit: courtesy atopos: architecture<>urbanism

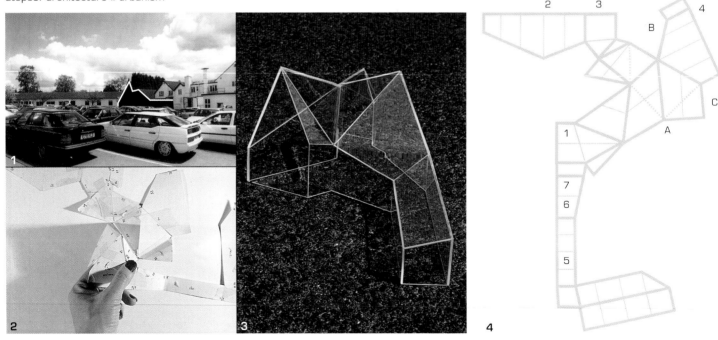

Walton Heath Golf Club, Surrey, UK: Transformation of a previously closed, elite organization into a corporate club and sports center, using minimal means to change how patrons move from entrance to parking lot to clubhouse to golf course. 1 Montage of new glass entrance concourse as "hole." Glass "envelope" will enclose space between the two buildings to create an electronic communications concourse with information displays, video, and ATM facilities. A new grass-green asphalt surface forms both car park and floor of the new building; 2 Folding the envelope; 3 Study model of glass envelope, with folded forms producing multiple effects of reflected light; 4 Envelope diagram (key: A–C: bent glass valley sections; 1–7: cantilevered glass panels). Photo credit: courtesy atopos: architecture<>urbanism

Costantini Museum, Buenos Aires, Argentina: 1 Section through museum/park assemblage. Programs of public plaza and private museum are folded together, producing topological continuities with traffic infrastructure and accelerating the emergence of the surrounding district as a regional, cultural, and entertainment center. "Outside" is continuous with "inside," reinforced through the organization of space, surfaces, materials, and so on. Water, sound, and lighting effects are altered by changes in surrounding environment (such as fluctuations in traffic flow); 2 Model view across park/pampas; 3 Computer model of entrance area; 4 Computer model of view across park; 5 Aerial view. Photo credit: courtesy atopos: architecture<>urbanism; physical model by Capital Models, London

1

Hotel Lago Espejo, Argentina: A hotel composed of four long buildings formed in a continuously looping skin of concrete and wood, exaggerating the effects of containment and exposure. Trees grow through this surface and small glass lenses allow light to pass through it. Private guest rooms are contemplative spaces with light but no views; public areas are vast, with a heightened sense of openness and continuity with the surrounding landscape. 1&2 Views of the hotel as a synthetic landscape; 3 Bifurcating surface and dynamic equilibrium study; 4 Montage-view from lake. Photo credit: courtesy atopos: architecture<>urbanism

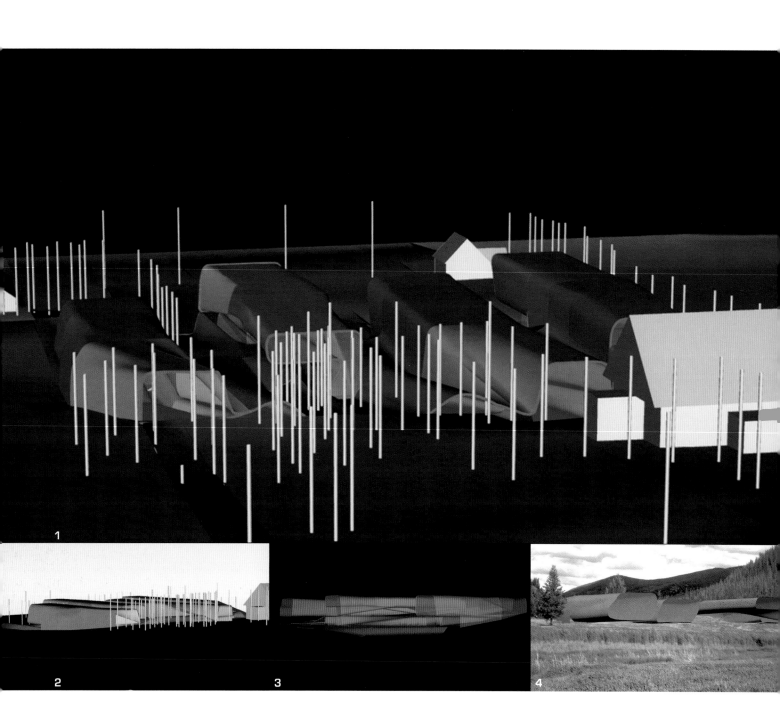

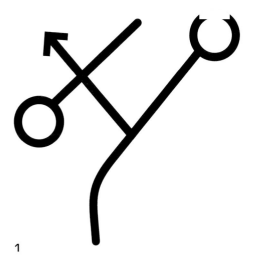

Better Living Terrain, Bournville, Birmingham, UK: 1 Diagram of miniaturized suburban layout/full-size installation redesigning the central courtyard of a suburban art school according to the operational logic of an existing service yard; 2 View across courtyard. Construction was completed in 48 hours, using a combination of road-building technology and the techniques of typical home improvement television shows; 3 View of terrain from entrance archway. Photo credit: courtesy atopos: architecture<>urbanism

Itsuko Hasegawa
Japan

*"When I design a building, I design not only the structure but also the
'program' of the building, everything that will affect the experiences
and activities of the people who use the building."*

PROFESSIONAL HISTORY

After Itsuko Hasegawa graduated from the Department of Architecture at Kanto Gakuin University in 1964, she practiced with Kiyonori Kikutake Architect & Associates until 1969. From 1969 to 1978, she practiced at the Tokyo Institute of Technology, first as a research student in the Department of Architecture and later with the Kazuo Shinohara Atelier. In 1979 she founded Itsuko Hasegawa Atelier in Tokyo.

Hasegawa is sought after as a lecturer and speaker. She has been a lecturer at Waseda University in Tokyo and at Tokyo University of Technology, and in 1992–1993 was a visiting professor at Harvard University's Graduate School of Design. In 1997 she was made an honorary fellow of the Royal Institute of British Architects.

Selected Awards

Building Contractor's Society Prize, for Shonandai Cultural Center, 1992

Cultural Award for Residential Architecture (Fukuoka, Japan), 1991

Avon Arts Award, 1990

Design Prize, Architectural Institute of Japan, 1986

Fujisawa Cultural Design Award, for the Shonandai Cultural Center, 1986

Japan's Cultural Design Award, Japan Inter-Design Forum, 1986

Selected Publications

Pollock, Naomi. "Niigata Performing Arts Center." *Architectural Record*, May 1999.

Itsuko Hasegawa: Selected and Current Works. Mulgrave, Australia: The Images Publishing Group, 1997.

Scheou, Anne, ed. *Itsuko Hasegawa: Recent Buildings and Projects*. Basel, Switzerland: Birkhauser, 1997.

Hasegawa, Itsuko. *Itsuko Hasegawa* (Architectural Monograph, No. 31). London: Academy Editions, 1993.

"The Complete Works of Itsuko Hasegawa." *Space Design*, April 1985.

FIRM PROFILE

Itsuko Hasegawa Atelier was formed in 1979. In the two decades since, the firm has gained national and international recognition, with projects ranging from cultural, medical, and academic facilities to residential structures, commercial buildings, and landscape architecture. After the Japanse government became an important patron of architecture in the late 1980s, the practice won a number of important commissions to design government-sponsored projects, including Urban Scape in Shiogama

(1989), the Kurahashi-Machi Town Center in Hiroshima (1995), the Shiogama City Town Center in Miyagi (1995), the Ishihara Public Housing Rebuilding Project (1996), and the Fukuroi City Town Center (1997), as well as those illustrated on pages 88–91.

Itsuko Hasegawa Atelier, which has been called a "visionary" firm by many observers, has a rare ability to create designs that incorporate the latest in design and construction technology and at the same time respect national cultural traditions, local diversity, and site-specific environmental conditions. A profile of Hasegawa posted on the Microsoft Web site said that her "projects are appreciated by all people as buildings that invite, inspire, and unite the human experience with the environment." Hasegawa herself often describes specific designs in metaphorical terms, making connections between architecture, art, and the natural world.

DESIGN STATEMENT

Architecture as extended metaphor

Although the Niigata Performing Arts Center project was an extremely complex project, Itsuko Hasegawa has long sought a simple metaphor to summarize its fundamental concept. Recently, she has been using the term "island hopping"— with its imagery of flight and loose, nonlinear movement—for this purpose. As opposed to more closed systems, "island hopping" implies a choice of paths, of connections and "disconnections," a freedom that Hasegawa strives to incorporate into her architecture. Translated into a landscape, it might be interpreted in the guise of floating green islands, or archipelagos, another metaphor.

Over the past ten years, consideration of the waterfront transition zone between port and city has been an important part of Hasegawa's work. Studying these complex edges, with their plurality of life, unique rhythms, and involved interrelationships, has given rise to an understanding of how these properties might relate to architecture itself. From this research came the aforementioned "island hopping" concept, in which the process of making architecture is likened to the formation of an archipelago, an eccentric island pattern. It is a poetic act, similar in spirit to the composition and performance of music.

In the case of the Yamanashi Fruit Museum, Hasegawa Atelier began with a concept and image sketch of flying fruit seeds just landed on the ground. These shapes, like rolling dewdrops on a lotus

leaf, were then translated into glass domes—natural shapes that express the balance between gravity and the surface tension present in a water droplet. Water ripples produced by wind, and other water metaphors, became a model for the architecture. It might be said that the competition model for the Niigata project is an extension of this imagery, taking on the form of seven water droplets.

ILLUSTRATED PROJECTS

Niigata City Performing Arts Center, Niigata, Japan, 1998: An arts center surrounded by six floating gardens, with elevated walkways connecting the gardens and center. At the north end, a glass wall protects the façade from the sun, its design inspired by a type of screen used at outdoor Japanese festivals. The performance centers, including a 2000-seat concert hall, 280-seat Noh theater, and 900-seat theater, were grouped under one roof to maximize the space available for landscape design.

Museum of Fruit, Yamanashi, Japan, 1995: The structures of the museum are a metaphor for the fecundity and diversity of fruit: the greenhouse evokes the tropical sun, which allows seeds to germinate; large trees in the plaza are the final stage in one cycle and the beginning of a new cycle. The buildings are of different sizes, materials, and orientation with respect to the terrain, either planted firmly in the earth or seemingly about to fly away.

STM House, Shibuya, Tokyo, Japan, 1991: The metaphor for the STM house is a rainbow. The façade of the building changes colors depending on one's viewpoint and on weather conditions. The rainbow "serpent" which undulates in the daytime disappears into the urban background at twilight, then returns as a pure white entity when the lights inside the building are turned on at night.

Sumida Culture Factory, Sumida, Tokyo, Japan, 1994: The building's volume is distributed in three major blocks around a central plaza, connected to one another by eight bridges. These bridges and a series of see-through elevators promote visual connections and provide a unique kinesthetic experience.

Shonandai Cultural Center, Fujisawa, Kanagawa, Japan, 1990: The guiding concept for this project was "architecture as latent nature." Seventy percent of the floor area is underground, leaving as much ground space as possible for outdoor gardens and a large plaza. An interior sunken garden and extensive roof gardens further emphasize the interconnectedness between man and nature.

Niigata City Performing Arts Center, Niigata, Japan: 1&2 Two of the six floating gardens that surround the arts center and some of the elevated walkways; 3 Night view of the east facade of the center; at the right can be seen part of the curtain wall; 4 Longitudinal section of 2000-seat concert hall, 280-seat Noh theater, and 900-seat theater; 5 Main lobby, second floor; 6 The main lobby, which at its greatest height is 39 feet, is open all day, whether or not performances are taking place; 7 Detail of curtain wall; 8 View down rake of the larger of the two theaters. Photo credits: Katsuhisa Kida [1–3, 5, 6]; Misumasa Fujitsuka [7&8]

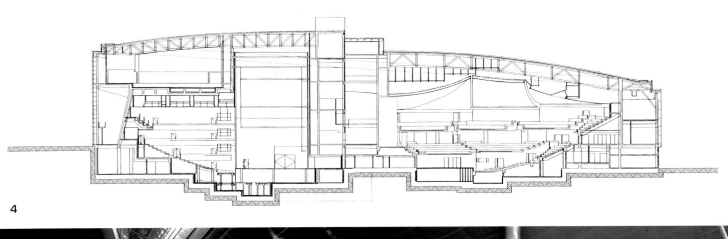

4

5

6

7

8

[Below] **Museum of Fruit, Yamanashi, Japan:** 1 Workshop plan; 2 Aerial view at night, showing crystal "seeds" as though landing on the landscape; 3 Leaf House with ceiling designed as a light "leaf"; 4 Roof terrace. Steel frame is designed to be covered with ivy. Photo credits: Mitsumasa Fujitsuka [2, 4]; Taisuke Ogawa [3]

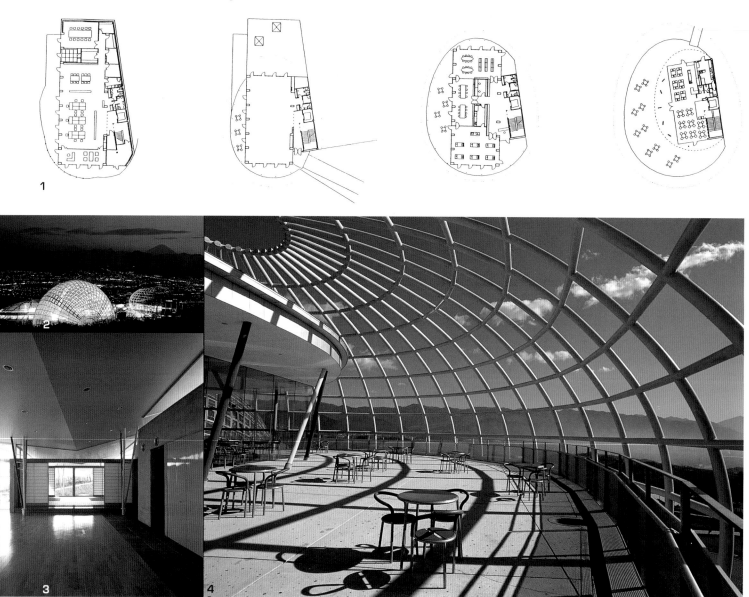

1

[Above] **STM House, Shibuya, Tokyo, Japan:** 1 Exterior, showing facade as a transparent interface with the street; 2 Night view, with building lit from within and glowing like a lantern; 3 Glass sliding doors reduce the separation between interior and exterior. Photo credit: Mitsumasa Fujitsuka

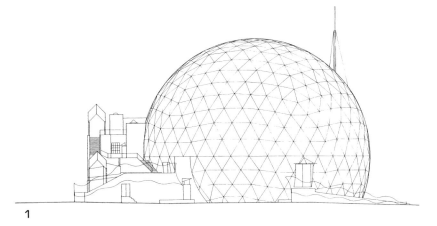

[Below] **Sumida Culture Factory, Sumida, Tokyo, Japan:** 1 Night view; 2 Outer screen. The exterior of the building is wrapped with perforated metal; 3 Interior of audio-visual room on third floor. Photo credits: Mitsumasa Fujitsuka [1]; Taisuke Ogawa [2]; courtesy Itsuko Hasegawa [3]

1

2

3

1

2

3

[Above] **Shonandai Cultural Center, Fujisawa, Kanagawa, Japan:** 1 Plan of north elevation; 2 West elevation; 3 View of children's space across the plaza. Photo credit: Shuji Yamada

Laurie Hawkinson
United States of America

"Indeterminacy is a fact of life."

PROFESSIONAL HISTORY

Laurie Hawkinson received a bachelor of fine arts in 1974 and a master's of fine arts in 1975 from the University of California, Berkeley. From 1976 to 1980 she attended the Independent Study Program at the Whitney Museum in New York City, and from 1978 to 1980 was director of exhibitions for New York's Institute for Architecture and Urban Studies. In 1983 she received a bachelor's degree in architecture from The Cooper Union in New York City.

In 1983 she and Henry Smith-Miller co-founded Smith-Miller + Hawkinson Architects, a New York-based architecture and urban planning firm. Currently she sits on the board of directors of the Wooster Group, an ensemble of artists who collaborate on the development and production of theater and media pieces, and the board of directors of New York City's Architectural League. She is an associate professor and is the core studio director of Columbia University's Graduate School of Architecture.

Laurie Hawkinson has practiced at and contributed to Peer Professional, General Services Administration, Public Building Service and Design Excellence Program, Washington, D.C., as well as design programs at the Southern California Institute of Architecture, Yale University, Columbia University, Harvard University's Graduate School of Design, the Parsons School of Design, and at the Institute for Advanced Architectural Studies in Venice, Italy.

Selected Awards

United States Institute for Theater Technology Honor Award, for the Performing Arts Theater at the Corning Glass Center, 1998

Art Commission of the City of New York, The 15th Annual Awards for Excellence in Design, for the Wall Street Ferry Pier, 1997

United States Institute for Theater Technology Honor Award, for the North Carolina Museum of Art Amphitheater and Outdoor Cinema, 1997

American Institute of Architects (AIA) New York Project Award, for Mixed-Use Building, Seoul, Korea, 1996

AIA New York Architecture Citation, for the NCMA Amphitheater and Outdoor Cinema, 1996

AIA New York Chapter Interior Architecture Award, for the Hetrick Martin Institute, 1994

New York State/AIA Design Award, for the Rotunda Gallery, 1993

AIA Design Award, for Private Residence, 1990

Selected Publications

Between Spaces: Smith-Miller + Hawkinson Architecture. The Princeton Architectural Press, 2000.

Ockman, Joan (ed.). "Spectacle." *Casabella,* 1999–2000.

Cramer, Ned. "Smith-Miller + Hawkinson's Crystalline Addition to the Corning Museum of Glass." *Architecture,* September 1999.

"House of Pane." *Metropolis,* November 1999.

"The Corning Glass Center." *Architectural Record,* September 1998.

Museum Architecture. North Carolina Museum of Art, Rockport Publishers (NCMA), 1998.

"The Corning Glass Center: Where Innovators Have Captured the Aura of Glass." *New York Times* Architecture Section, 14 June, 1998.

Betsky, Aaron. "An Enforced Minimalism: The Work of Smith-Miller + Hawkinson." *ARCHIS,* September 1997: 36–45.

"Points of View: New Line Cinema East/ New Line Cinema West." *Architectural Record,* September 1992.

FIRM PROFILE

Smith-Miller + Hawkinson Architects has designed and executed public and private projects across the United States, ranging from residential commissions to parks, corporate buildings, and museums. The firm's guiding principles are derived from an ongoing investigation into the general culture of architecture—its history as well as its complex and changing relationship to society and contemporary ideas. Since its inception in 1983, the office of Smith-Miller + Hawkinson has maintained a deep commitment to research in all of its architectural projects, both built and unbuilt, and indeed has become a laboratory for both research and practice.

Collaboration is an essential aspect of the way in which Smith-Miller + Hawkinson Architects works. Collaboration operates not only among architects, but also cuts across hierarchies and disciplines in the firm's work with artists, landscape architects, and structural engineers. At a time when there are no simple answers to questions of "style" or even to the future of architecture, such a collaborative approach helps to broaden the definitions of both architecture and architect and has allowed the firm to engage in productive overlaps with other fields that are undergoing similar critical inquiries.

Smith-Miller + Hawkinson's work was featured at the 1996 Venice Bienniale for Architecture, and has been exhibited at

the Museum of Modern Art, New York; the Centre Georges Pompidou in Paris, France; and the Deutsches Architektur Museum in Germany. *The New York Times* described Smith-Miller + Hawkinson's work as "proof that craftsmanship, technology and cutting-edge architecture can live happily under one roof." The firm has received international attention for an outdoor cinema and the North Carolina Museum of Art Amphitheater, designed with artist Barbara Kruger and landscape architect Nicholas Quennell.

Selected Clients

Battery Park City Authority
Continental Airlines
Cornell University
Corning Inc.
New Line Cinema
New York City Police Museum
North Carolina Museum of Art
Princeton University
RGA Digital Studios
Samsung Corporation

DESIGN STATEMENT

The Corning Museum of Glass, which opened in upstate New York in June 1999, represents Smith-Miller + Hawkinson's investigations into the meaning of glass as an architectural material.

The entry façade at the main entrance to the Corning Glass Center is comprised of a curtain wall that utilizes a mullionless, point-fitting system, together with a series of very thin, light stainless steel vertical trusses placed both inside and outside the building to challenge the idea of perimeter. Contrary to typical curtain-wall construction, the visitor does not enter the exhibit hall at right angles to the façade, but rather between and parallel to it. The purposeful and deliberate display of structure and glass plate celebrates the visitors' passage from exterior to interior, and serves to reveal the exploratory nature of the Glass Center itself. Inside, the circulation is nonlinear throughout. Nothing was left to chance. The ubiquitous glass pieces were all deliberately designed to be out of plumb or nonorthogonal, creating constantly shifting patterns of color and reflectivity.

ILLUSTRATED PROJECTS

Corning Museum of Glass, Corning, New York, 1999

North Carolina Museum of Art, Raleigh, North Carolina, 1996

Greenberg Loft, New York City, 1997

(Left) **North Carolina Museum of Art, Amphitheater, Raleigh, North Carolina:** 1 Canopy over stage with projection house beyond; 2 Detail. Photo credits: Paul Warchol (1); Judith Turner (2)

(Above) **Greenberg Loft, New York City:** 1 Stair; 2 Stair up to second level; 3 Detail of railing at mezzanine.
Photo credits: Michael Moran (1&2); Judith Turner (3)

(Left) **Corning Museum of Glass, Corning, New York:** 1 Curtain wall; 2 South façade; 3 Orientation theater; 4 Visitor Center entry; 5 Lobby; 6 Café. Photo credits: Judith Turner (1&2); Paul Warchol (3-6)

Christine Hawley
United Kingdom

"One of the great bonuses of design is that it is a social activity. I would like to think that we understand the obvious, but actually we get great pleasure out of pursuing the alternative, particularly if it offers a better solution."

PROFESSIONAL HISTORY

Christine Hawley completed her Architectural Association Diploma at the Architectural Association School of Architecture, London, in 1975. While she was completing her studies, she worked in the Department of Environment in London and practiced with Renton, Howard, Wood and Levin Architects, also in London. From 1972 to 1973 she practiced with De Soissons Partnership Architects and Yorke Rosenberg and Mardell (YRM) Architects, both in London.

In 1975, Hawley became a partner in Cook and Hawley Architects, London. In 1978 she registered as a British architect (ARCUK) and practiced with Pearson International Architects in London. In 1998 she established Christine Hawley Architects, also in London.

Hawley's academic career is long and distinguished. From 1979 to 1987 she taught at the Architectural Association School of Architecture, and from 1987 to 1993 she was head of the University of East London School of Architecture (formerly PEL). In 1993 she became a professor of architectural studies at London's Bartlett School of Architecture, Building, Environmental Design and Planning, and in 1999 was made dean of faculty of the built environment and head of school at Bartlett, the largest graduate school specializing in the built environment in the UK.

Hawley has been a member of the Royal Institute of British Architects (RIBA) since 1982 and a fellow since 1983. Currently, she is a member of the Design Review Committee of the Commission for Architecture and the Built Environment, established in 1999.

Selected Awards

Royal Institute of British Architects Teaching Award, 1998–1999

Visiting Chair of Design, The Technical University, Vienna, 1997

Visiting Chair of Design, Oslo University, 1992

Selected Publications

"Debating Domesticity." *Architectural Design*, May/June 1999.

"Gifu Kitagata Apartments." *Architecture and Design*, June 1999.

Finch, Paul. "A Woman's Place." *Architects' Journal*, May 28, 1998.

"Peter Cook and Christine Hawley." Special Issue, *Architecture + Urbanism*, February 1980.

FIRM PROFILE

Cook and Hawley Architects, established in 1975 as a partnership between Christine Hawley and Peter Cook, began with a number of small domestic projects in Europe and the Far East. During the 1980s, the practice developed strong links with Germany, initially designing a series of solar houses in Rhineland Pfalz, and winning competition prizes for the DOM Lock Headquarters and Hochst Spars Hall, the Elbberg Offices, and one of the last blocks of social housing to be built for the International Bauausstellung at Lützoplatz. During the same period, several strategic planning studies were undertaken for the Hamburg docks; a stained glass museum in Langan, Germany; and a glass pavilion for the Städel Academy in Frankfurt partnership.

Christine Hawley Architects, founded in 1998 by Christine Hawley, has a project list that ranges from corporate and commercial spaces to educational, leisure, and cultural facilities; environmental planning; landscaping; and residential. The practice has won prizes in several competitions, including the Living Sites Competition and the Salford Crescent Master Planning and Landscaping Competition. The International Congress Center for the EUR district, Rome, was also a prize-winning design.

Current projects at Christine Hawley Architects include the second phase of a 120-unit block of social housing being constructed in Gifu, Japan, and the design for a museum of Roman antiquities in Bad Deutsch-Altenberg, Austria, commissioned by the Lower Austrian Government, to be constructed in 2002 (see pages 98–101).

DESIGN STATEMENT

Kitagata Housing Reconstruction, Gifu, Japan / Christine Hawley Architects

The project was initiated to develop a critique of social housing in Japan, the plans of which are used as universal templates and have remained unchanged since 1945. In contrast, the structure and lifestyle of the Japanese family has experienced accelerated change over the past fifty years. The initial discussion addressed changes in family structure and how they might affect housing design in the future.

Of particular interest to Christine Hawley Architects was how we might reconcile the requirements of a developing lifestyle with spatial adaptability. How could space be characterized to overcome the relentless anonymity of public housing? What is the qualitative, rather than the quantitative, value of space? Initial proposals incorporated flexible wall systems, mobile elements, and courtyards that could become extensions of the living space. An early decision to organize the apartments as duplexes offered an opportunity to comfortably separate the more communal areas from the private areas, and to prescribe the spatial organization of the building.

The sculptural form was, in part, characterized by context: the perimeter contours of the site. This, together with the geometry of the internal plane, was abstracted and formed the base of the blue relief on the building. As the building is large, I felt it important to characterize the external form rather than produce a monolithic, repetitive facade.

Internally, most apartments are arranged as duplexes with the larger, open communal spaces on the lower level. Above are the bedrooms, some with views down into the living area. Several apartments have double-height space and all have vertical stairwells that, together with the arrangement of windows, accelerate air movement through the apartments. All have balconies and specially designed "futon" rails that allow futons to be aired during the day.

ILLUSTRATED PROJECTS

Kitagata Housing Reconstruction, Gifu, Japan, 1994–2000

IBA Housing, Berlin, 1986–1990

Salford Master Planning and Landscaping Museum, Manchester, UK, 1999

Städel Academy Canteen, Frankfurt, Germany, 1989–1991

Hix Sac Loqvvntvr Pfaffenberg Museum Extension, Bad Deutsch-Altenberg, Austria, 1993–2001

International Congress Center, Rome, 1998

Osaka Folly, Osaka, Japan, 1989–1990

Kitagata Housing Reconstruction, Gifu, Japan: 1 Exterior view of front; 2 Detail of front elevation showing concrete facade with painted elements, perforated aluminum balconies, and futon rails; 3 Rear view at night, highlighting the sculptural form of the building, the external public walkways that are held off the facade, and the internal stairwells of the duplex apartments; 4 Interior view showing the entrance bridge, sculpted balustrade, and view out to the landscaped courtyard through the double-height glazing. Photo credit: Tomio Ohashi

4

IBA Housing, Berlin, Germany: 1 Simple rear facade with set-back balconies; 2 Detail of rear facade, showing articulated drain pipe; 3 Front elevation, showing highly sculpted winter gardens. Photo credit: courtesy Christine Hawley Architects

[Right] **Salford Master Planning and Landscaping Museum, Manchester, UK:** Computer model of proposal to improve and develop the Salford Crescent area in Salford, both in terms of infrastructure and landscape, using hard and soft landscaping, illumination, and building. Photo credit: courtesy Christine Hawley Architects

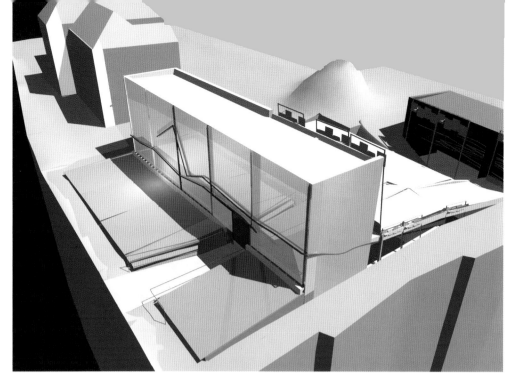

[Above] **Hix Sac Loqvvntvr Pfaffenberg Museum Extension, Bad Deutsch-Altenberg, Austria:**
Computer model showing added exhibition and café space. Photo credit: Christine Hawley Architects

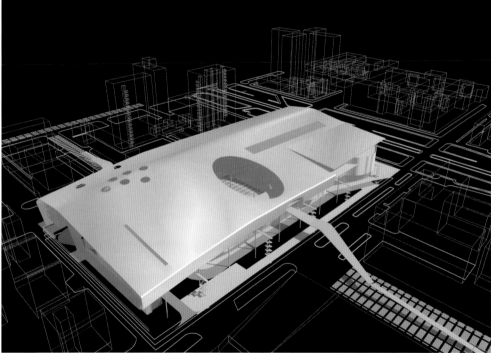

[Above] **International Congress Center, Rome:** Computer model. The skin is broken only by points
of public entry and to indicate significant events. Photo credit: courtesy Christine Hawley Architects

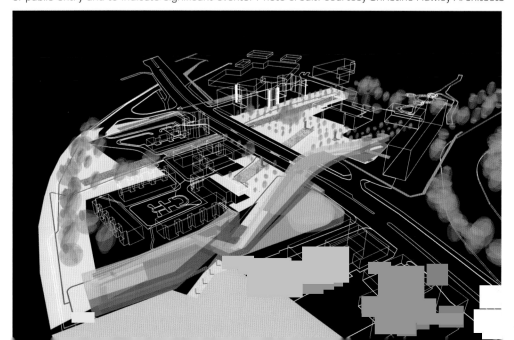

[Below] **Städel Academy Canteen, Frankfurt, Germany:** Exterior view of small canteen and exhibition space for art school. Two-thirds of roof canopy opens along its entire length, allowing for rapid cooling and exposure to open air in summer. Photo credit: courtesy Christine Hawley Architects

[Above] **Osaka Folly, Osaka, Japan:**
1&2 Exterior views. Austere metal facade faces a busy public concourse; every two minutes water pours from the structure's base, moving the yellow wand. The mechanism is revealed inside, where a thin veil of water constantly runs over a large glass plane, collecting in a receptacle and then tipping through the facade every two minutes. Photo credit: courtesy Christine Hawley Architects

Margaret Helfand
United States of America

"Architecture can spring directly from the process by which it is made, with a minimum of elaboration."

PROFESSIONAL HISTORY

Margaret Helfand received her master's in architecture from the University of California in 1973 after studying at the College of Environmental Design, Berkeley, and the Architectural Association in London. After graduating she worked with Archigram in London. From 1976 to 1981 she was an associate with Marcel Breuer Associates in New York City, and in 1981 she created her own practice, Margaret Helfand Architects, where she was sole principal. In 1999, Helfand Myerberg Guggenheimer was formed.

Helfand has served as a planning and design consultant for the City of New York and for the University of California in San Francisco. She often serves as guest critic in architecture studios at Columbia University, Pratt Institute, SCI-Arc (Southern California Institute of Architecture), Yale University, and the University of Pennsylvania. In 2000 she was a vice president of the New York Chapter of the American Institute of Architects (AIA). In 2001, she became president of AIA New York Chapter and treasurer of the New York Foundation for Architecture. She has been a fellow of AIA since 1998.

Helfand is licensed in New York, New Jersey, Connecticut, and Pennsylvania. She has an international reputation for innovative approaches to a wide range of building types, interiors, and products, and her work has been featured in several retrospectives.

Selected Awards

AIA New York Chapter Distinguished Architecture Award, for Kohlberg Hall at Swarthmore College, 1998

AIA New York Chapter Distinguished Architecture Project Award, for Lt. Petrosino Park, 1996

AIA New York Chapter Distinguished Architecture Award, for Pakatakan Industrial Building, 1992

Selected Publications

Helfand, Margaret et. al. *Margaret Helfand Architects: Essential Architecture*. New York: Monacelli Press, 1999.

Hine, Thomas. "Margaret Helfand's Kohlberg Hall." *Architectural Record*, February 1997.

McGuire, Penny. "Time In." *Architectural Review*, April 1997.

Vercelloni, M. *Urban Interiors in New York & USA*. Milan: Edizioni L'Archivolto, 1996.

Freiman, Ziva. "Joint Effort" [Bronx Community College Child Development Center]. *Progressive Architecture*, March 1995.

Russell, Beverly. *Women of Design: Contemporary American Interiors*. New York: Rizzoli, 1992.

FIRM PROFILE

Founded in 1999 and positioned to lead in the new century, Helfand Myerberg Guggenheimer is a twenty-two-person architecture, planning, and interiors firm that advances the needs and visions of its clients.

The firm's partners and staff offer considerable expertise in high-profile design for institutional, corporate, cultural, commercial, and residential clients, developed over the past two decades in three preceding firms headed respectively by Margaret Helfand (1981–1999), Henry Myerberg (1986–1999), and Peter Guggenheimer (1991–1999).

The new firm merges the highest levels of science (CAD, building sciences, business) and art (logic, beauty, simplicity) to create a modern practice of architecture, run by partners with a long history of delivering high-quality design and management services on time and on budget. Helfand Myerberg Guggenheimer enjoys the patronage of many repeat clients, including all those listed below.

Selected Clients

Bryn Mawr College
Calvin Klein
City University of New York
Cornell University
Home Box Office (HBO)
Ian Schrager
Levi's Dockers
Museum of American Folk Art
Nina Footwear
Swarthmore College
Time Out New York magazine

DESIGN STATEMENT

All architectural projects share the same challenge: to solve physical needs in real time and real space, and with real materials. Each designer must develop her or his own strategy for approaching this task.

The work of Helfand Myerberg Guggenheimer relies on a design strategy based on the three axes of thought essential to architecture: geometry, structure, and materials. Its design decisions are guided by the desire to minimize elaboration, letting the geometry, structure, and materials of each project speak for themselves, thereby creating an architecture distinguished by its logic, simplicity, and sensuality.

Geometry

Any design solution must begin with a commitment to some form of order. Helfand Myerberg Guggenheimer's projects spring from the geometry appropriate to each project, whether it be Cartesian geometry (as in the Industrial Park Building, page 107) or asymmetry responding to site conditions or program (as in the Cloister for Learning, page 106). As each project develops, the internal logic of the materials employed creates another layer of order. The resulting forms are often basic geometric shapes that can be easily identified with the form of the raw materials from which they are built.

Structure

Architecture is made of matter and, therefore, needs a logic of structure to exist in space. Structure can contribute eloquently to architectural form, from the overall building structure (the Industrial Park Building) to the smallest scale of detail (the granite column cladding at the Cloister for Learning) or functional object incorporated into a project (the bent steel tables in the Architects' Offices project, pages 104–105).

Materials

Materials are the matter from which architecture is made. In the firm's work, materials are selected for their structural, visual, and tactile properties, with an eye to cost. Often, innovative applications of materials evolve from budget or schedule constraints (such as the homosote wall in the Architects' Office and the metal canopy at the entrance to Industrial Park Building). Materials, shaped by concepts of geometry and structure, represent the ultimate reality of each project to the observer, and thus can communicate deep emotive properties.

ILLUSTRATED PROJECTS

Architects' Offices, New York City, 1999

Industrial Park Building, Arkville, New York, 1990

Cloister for Learning, Swarthmore, Pennsylvania, 1996

Architects' Offices, New York City: 1 Partner's office framed by translucent polycarbonate screen wall with view of Soho; 2 Rotating glass-panel entry door with bent bronze pull, defining floor plan of office; 3 A large conference room, animated by bent steel-plate table and chairs, joining the two wings of the office; 4 Individual workstations along a row of north-facing windows; 5 Reception area. Photo credit: Paul Warchol Photography

1
2
3
4

Katharine Heron
United Kingdom

"The most important thing is to get the relationship with the client right."

PROFESSIONAL HISTORY

Katharine Heron studied at the Architectural Association from 1965 to 1972. She practiced with James Cubit & Partners from 1966 to 1967, with Robert Matthew Johnson-Marshall & Partners from 1972 to 1973, and with Levit Bernstein Associates from 1975 to 1979. During the 1970s she held part-time teaching appointments at the Architectural Association, NELP, SLP, and the University of Westminster. From 1974 to 1976 she worked as a partner with Leon van Schaik. In 1977, she co-founded Mudchute Park & Farm, where she was director until 1984. In 1984 Heron and Julian Feary co-founded Feary + Heron Architects, London.

In addition to her work as a practicing architect, Heron has always been committed to a wide range of academic pursuits, as well as advisory and committee posts in various architecture- and design-related organizations. In 1994 she was professional studies course leader at the University of Westminster, and in 1997–1998 made important contributions to the British Design Council's "Creative Britain" initiative. Currently she is external examiner at EUL and UNL (since 1995), and a member of the Arts Council of England's Visual Arts Panel, Architecture Group (since 1996; chair since 1998). She has been chair of the Arts Council Architecture Group since 1998 and chair of the Department of Architecture, University of Westminster, since 1997.

Selected Awards

First Prize, Casabella Competition, "City as a Significant Environment," 1982

Civic Trust Museum of the Year Award, 1980

Come to Britain Trophy and Royal Institute of British Architects Commendation, 1980

Selected Publications

Heron, Patrick. *Colour in Space: Patrick Heron, Public Projects.* St. Ives: Tate Gallery, 1999.

Contemporary British Architects. New York: Prestel, 1994.

"Kate Heron." *Architectural Review,* December 1991.

FIRM PROFILE

Feary + Heron Architects is a small practice with a wide range of experience. The two principals are wife and husband. Their work has involved designing residences; developing innovative structures and prototypes using new technology; landscape design; furniture and exhibition design; collaborative work with artists; conversion of existing buildings for new uses; gallery design, including alteration and renovation; writing briefs; and finding sites. Because Feary + Heron works on such a wide range of project types, the firm has developed the ability to satisfy disparate clients' needs—whether the client is a wheelchair-bound working mother (the technically demanding Keith Schofield House, London) or a crafts organization with a low budget and a need to take the finished designs on tour (exhibition designs done for the Crafts Council).

Whatever the project, Feary + Heron Architects seeks to maintain the accessibility, flexibility, and attention to detail that are the traditional virtues of the small practice and, at the same time, embrace new technologies—through both research and practice—that support large and more complex projects. Right from a project's inception, the firm uses digital process and exchange to work closely and efficiently with consultants outside of London, both in the UK and internationally, whose creative input makes the design process truly interactive. The firm believes in, and practices, teamwork.

The partners have expertise in different areas. Julian Feary is the practice's "boiler room": He takes the lead in design and technical issues and delights in all the aspects of construction necessary for the successful realization of design ideas. Katharine Heron's extensive teaching and committee work ensure that the office keeps abreast of current architectural concerns in professional practice, computer-aided design, and theory. This supports the practice's drive to research and develop new materials and techniques and maintains an awareness of the wider political, cultural, and social concerns.

Selected Clients

Arkwright Arts Trust
Arts for Health
Barbican Art Gallery
Cornwall County Council
Craftspace Touring
Henry Moore Foundation
International Musicians Seminar, Prussia Cove
Land Securities Properties Ltd.
London Borough of Southwark
London Docklands Development Corporation
Pier Arts Trust Oriel Cardiff
South West Arts
St. Stephens Walbrook
Waddington Galleries

DESIGN STATEMENT

All projects are challenging to design.

Every one is a one-off, and every one must meet the client's expectations and budget.

ILLUSTRATED PROJECTS

University of Westminster

Piers Arts Centre

Flexible Furniture

Big Painting Sculpture

(Above) **University of Westminster, London**

(Above) **Big Painting Sculpture** (1&2)

(Above) **Flexible Furniture**

Patty Hopkins
United Kingdom

"The craft of architecture is very hard. Architects' lives are completely wrapped up in their buildings. We never stop thinking about a design until everything is finished, and for long afterwards."

PROFESSIONAL HISTORY

Patty Hopkins received a diploma from the Architectural Association (AA) in 1968. In 1976, she co-founded Michael Hopkins and Partners, a London-based architectural practice, with her husband Michael Hopkins. Over the twenty-five years since, she has achieved recognition not only for her work with the practice but also for her contributions to professional organizations and schools of architecture.

In 1993, Hopkins was appointed an assessor for the Civic Trust Awards, given annually to outstanding examples of architectural and environmental design that benefit their local areas. In 1994, she was appointed external examiner for Oxford Brookes University, Faculty of Architecture, and was elected for membership in both the Arts Council National Lottery Advisory Board, which advises and assists the Arts Council regarding capital investment in the arts, and the Architectural Association 150 Campaign Board, launched to celebrate the birth of formal architectural education in Britain and to drive a major fundraising campaign for the AA.

In 1996, Hopkins received a doctorate of technology (*honoris causa*) from the London Guildhall University and was made an honorary fellow of the American Institute of Architects (AIA).

Selected Awards

[The awards given to Michael Hopkins and Partners' projects are legion. The list below cites only those awarded to the three projects illustrated in this book: the Fleet Velmead Infants School (Hampshire, UK); the Glyndebourne Opera House (East Sussex, UK); and the Queen's Building at Emmanuel College (Cambridge, UK).]

Civic Trust Award: for Fleet Velmead, 1998; for Glyndebourne, 1995

Royal Institute of British Architects (RIBA) Award for Architecture: for Fleet Velmead, 1998; for Queen's Building, 1996; for Glyndebourne, 1994

Structural Steel Award, the British Construction Steelwork Association, for Fleet Velmead, 1998

Carpenters Award, the Worshipful Company of Carpenters and the Timber Trade: for Queen's Building, 1997; for Glyndebourne, 1995

New Building Category Winner, Natural Stone Awards, Stone Federation of Great Britain, for Queen's Building, 1997

RIBA Architecture in Education Award, for Queen's Building, 1996

Royal Fine Art Commission (London)

Arts Building of the Year Award: for Queen's Building, 1996; for Glyndebourne, 1994

Financial Times Building of the Year Award, for Glyndebourne, 1995

British Construction Industry Award, for Glyndebourne, 1994

RIBA Gold Medal, awarded to Michael and Patty Hopkins, 1984

Selected Publications

"Patty Hopkins, Architect." *Country Life*, 13 March 1997.

Callaghan, Will. "Top Forty Women Architects." *RIBA Journal*, October 1996.

Davis, Colin. "Cambridge Credo." *Architectural Review*, February 1996.

Field, Marcus. "A House in the Country— Reinventing Structural Stone in Cambridge." *Architectural Journal*, June 1995.

Davies, Colin. "Glyndebourne." *Architectural Review*, June 1994.

FIRM PROFILE

Founded in 1976, Michael Hopkins and Partners aims to design innovative, cost-effective, and beautiful buildings that enable clients to make the most of their sites, programs, and budgets. The practice creates logical and clean designs, following the principle of "truth to materials and expression of structure," from which stems the aesthetic quality, efficiency, and popular appeal of its buildings. Since its creation, the practice has pioneered a series of strategies, including fabric roofs, lightweight structures, energy-efficient designs, the weaving of new structures into already existing ones, and the recycling of former industrial sites. Its contribution to architecture has been recognized in numerous design awards, RIBA's Royal Gold Medal in 1994, and a knighthood for Michael Hopkins.

Michael Hopkins and Partners has expanded over the years, becoming one of the largest architectural firms in the United Kingdom. Since 1984, the practice has worked from a site in Marylebone, London, which has grown into an office campus with drawing studios, offices, and a modeling workshop.

Michael Hopkins and Partners believes that the best buildings come from close cooperation between architect, client, and other members of the project team, the resulting dialogue establishing the parameters necessary for its design approach and synthesizing creative imagination with rational logic.

Selected Clients (illustrated projects not included)

Bristol 2000 Ltd.

David Mellor Design Ltd.

The Dynamic Earth Charitable Trust

The Governors of Sutton Hospital in Charterhouse

The Haberdashers' Company

Manchester City Council

The Royal Academy of Arts

DESIGN STATEMENT

The Glyndebourne Opera House

The Glyndebourne opera is an institution that has developed over many years. It brings a cosmopolitan urban art form into an attractive urban setting. For this commission, completed in 1994, the architects had to increase the size of the existing facilities, improving conditions and at the same time ensuring that the sense and theater of the operatic experience was not overwhelmed. It was important to maintain the enchantment and the tradition.

The new building is in the same location as the previous one, although it has been turned 180 degrees to now face south to the garden. From a distance, one can see the new fly tower and roof, although the building is dug into a natural slope to reduce its apparent bulk so as to sit well with the main house and its surrounding buildings and continue the domestic, private-seeming nature of the site. There is no large front door or portico; instead, an open arcade welcomes arriving opera-goers.

Some of the architectural references are drawn from the practice's previous work: the round roof is similar to the circular, traditionally detailed lead-covered roof designed for David Mellor's Cutlery Factory in 1989; the fly tower has shades of the Schlumberger theater fly tower; and the canopy is a reminder of the tented canopy supported by the existing brick structure of the Mound Stand at Lord's Cricket Ground, London. Such echoes are inevitable—and desirable— when a practice follows at tight design direction, and the variety of projects that have been executed by following that direction are testaments to the enduring strength of the practice and its methodology.

ILLUSTRATED PROJECTS

Glyndebourne Opera House, East Sussex, UK, 1988–1994

The Queen's Building, Emmanuel College, Cambridge, UK, 1993–1995

Fleet Velmead Infants School, Hampshire, UK, 1984–1986

Glyndebourne Opera House, East Sussex, UK: 1 The semicircular backstage area, with stage and fly tower to the right; 2 The entrance canopy. As the building is only used during the summer, the foyer space is enveloped by a tensile canopy; 3 The pastoral vista from across the lake on the southeast side of the site; 4 The 1,200-seat auditorium has a gently raked bank of stalls and three horseshoe-shaped balconies. It is made from reclaimed pitch pine and brick. Photo credit: Martin Charles

[Right] **The Queen's Building, Emmanuel College, Cambridge, UK:**
1 Ground floor plan; 2 Longitudinal section; 3 Site plan.
Photo credit: courtesy Michael Hopkins and Partners

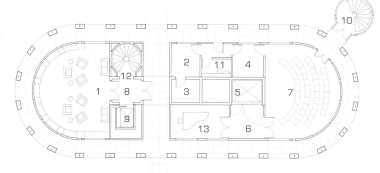

1

Fleet Velmead Infants School, Hampshire, UK: 1–3 All of
Fleet Velmead's classrooms open onto paved play areas where
teaching and activities can take place in the summer. Awnings
provide protection from the unwanted effects of glare and solar
gain. Photo credit: courtesy Michael Hopkins and Partners

Key
1   JCR reading room
2   Music practice room
3   Music store
4   Meeting/supervision room
5   Piano elevator
6   Lobby for piano elevator
7   Seminar/dressing room
8   Entrance lobby
9   Disabled elevator
10 Stairwell
11 WC
12 Main stair
13 Keyboard practice room

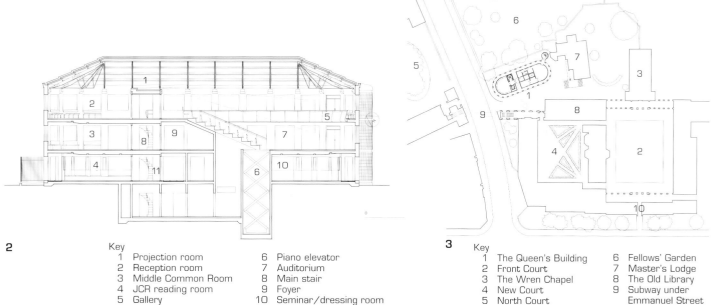

2

Key
1 Projection room
2 Reception room
3 Middle Common Room
4 JCR reading room
5 Gallery
6 Piano elevator
7 Auditorium
8 Main stair
9 Foyer
10 Seminar/dressing room
11 Main entrance

3

Key
1 The Queen's Building
2 Front Court
3 The Wren Chapel
4 New Court
5 North Court
6 Fellows' Garden
7 Master's Lodge
8 The Old Library
9 Subway under
   Emmanuel Street
10 Main entrance off
    St Andrew's Street

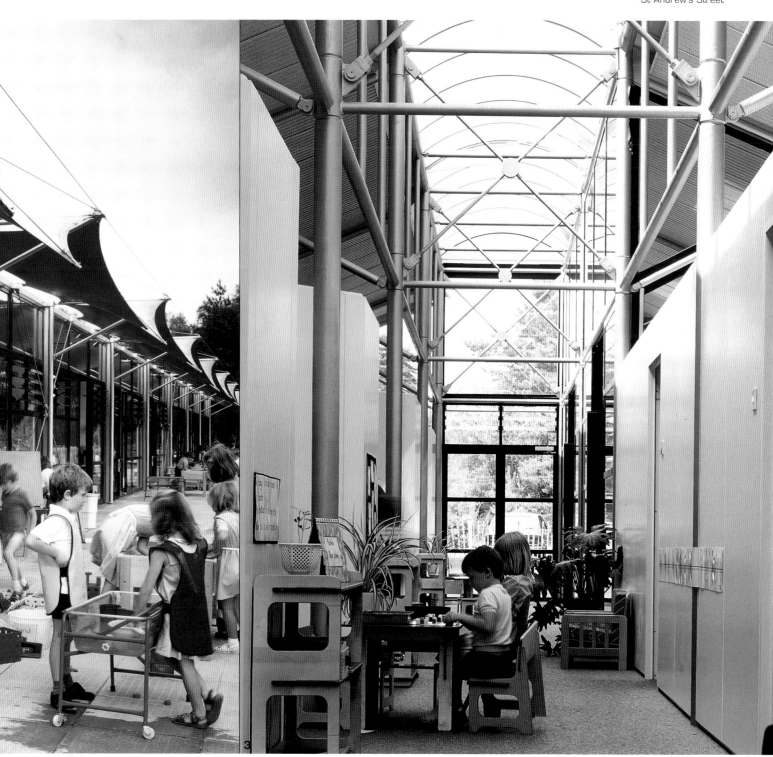

Cathi House

United States of America

"We look for moments of pause in the homes we create, those spaces that are not programmed—the surprises . . . and in each home they are different . . . that moment when you are between spaces, between thoughts, between activities—in which you can take a breath, remove your coat, change your mind—can be incredibly powerful."

PROFESSIONAL HISTORY

Cathi House received her bachelor of architecture degree in 1977 from Virginia Tech. After working with Wallace McHarg Roberts & Todd in Philadelphia, she took a year to travel and study in Europe, then moved to San Francisco and became an associate with architect Denis Shanagher. In 1980 she joined Marquis Associates on the team for San Francisco's innovative, award-winning Primate Discovery Center.

In 1982, House and her husband, Steven, established House + House Architects. There, she has contributed to a diverse body of work that demonstrates a passion for site-specific, well-choreographed homes throughout the San Francisco Bay Area, the Sierra Nevada mountains, Florida, Hawaii, Mexico, and the Caribbean.

Cathi House has been a visiting lecturer at universities throughout the United States. Since 1994 she has served on the Advisory Council for the College of Architecture and Urban Studies at Virginia Tech, and in 1999 was given the university's Award for Outstanding Professional Accomplishment in Architecture. An artist and photographer, her personal work includes ceramics, weaving, and clothing design.

Selected Awards

American Institute of Architects (AIA) San Francisco Bay Area Architectural Computer Graphics Award, 1999

Award for Outstanding Professional Accomplishment in Architecture, Virginia Tech University, 1999

Renaissance Design Award, 1999, 1997, 1993, 1991, *Remodeling* and the National Association of Home Builders

Met Home of the Year Award, *Metropolitan Home*, 1997

Berkeley Architectural Heritage Award, 1996

Builder's Choice Project of the Year Award, *Builder* and the National Association of Home Builders, 1996

AIA East Bay Design Award, 1995

American Society of Interior Designers (ASID) Design Excellence Award, 1995, 1993, 1992, 1991

Best in American Living Award, the National Association of Home Builders, 1994, 1989

Builder's Choice Design and Planning Award, 1994, 1991

Renaissance Design Project of the Year Award, 1993

Design Achievement Award, Design Industries Foundation for Aids, 1991, 1990

AIA Housing Merit Award, 1990

Selected Publications

Higgins, Lisa. "Casa Not Blanca." *Metropolitan Home*, January/February 1999.

House, Cathi and Steven. "A Courtyard House in Old Mexico." *Fine Homebuilding*, Spring 1999.

House, Cathi and Steven. *House Design: House + House Architects*. Monograph. Mulgrave, Australia: Images Publishing, 1999.

Bocchino, Rafaella. "Rifare la Corte." *Ville Giardini*, April 1998.

Lloyd, Peter. *San Francisco Houses After the Fire*. London: Ellipsis London, 1997.

FIRM PROFILE

House + House Architects endeavors to create beauty, serenity, and awe in its work. The firm's greatest inspiration comes from the subtleties of each site and the deepest recesses of its clients' souls. Through skillful manipulation of form, light, and texture, each project is molded into a unique, magical, and harmonious environment. The poetic quality of the work derives from the simpler side of life: the sparkle of sunlight touching a wall, the drama of surprise in turning a corner, the luminous glow of color at the moment of twilight.

House + House has received more than thirty design awards. In 1989 *Architecture* magazine selected the firm from more than 600 entries to feature in their "Discovery" issue on emerging talent. The firm's work has been exhibited widely and featured in national and international publications, including *Architecture*, *Architectural Record*, *House Beautiful*, *Metropolitan Home*, *Brava Casa*, *DBZ*, and *The New York Times*. Cathi and Steven House also created a major exhibition entitled "Mediterranean Indigenous Architecture: Timeless Solutions for the Human Habitat," a critical analysis of village architecture in Greece, Italy, Yugoslavia, and Spain.

DESIGN STATEMENT

A House for Two Architects, San Miguel de Allende, Mexico

After twenty-three years as a practicing architect, designing a home for myself and my husband in Mexico gave me the first opportunity to work without the constraints of a client but with the difficulties and opportunities of working in a foreign country, a foreign language, even a foreign scale. Our site measures only 37 feet by 52 feet (11 by 16.25 meters), in the center of a beautiful historic town in Mexico's central highlands. Working from thousands of miles away required precise drawings and the right builder. Careful research led me to a construction crew made up of true craftsmen; working with them was one of the great pleasures of my life.

Our home is a retreat, a place for personal growth, and a special place to share. Rooms fit together like a complex little village around a courtyard that fills every room with light and air. The journey between the spaces, and the vistas to and through them, give complexity to the form and a sense of dimension. In our work we often talk of choreographing space, moving through space not only physically but spiritually, emotionally, and visually, as well. Composition, proportion, movement, focus, vista, color, texture, and light to find wonder and joy, composing spaces to enhance life's journeys within the home.

Our travels have always been one of our great sources of inspiration, our spirits moved by a shaft of light raking a textured wall, a perfectly placed window, a surprise at the turn. Our home embodies much of the magic we have found in our travels and it renews our spirits.

ILLUSTRATED PROJECTS

A House for Two Architects, San Miguel de Allende, Mexico, 1996: The rooms, courtyard, balconies, and roof terraces of this house all interweave like a complex little village. Made entirely by hand and using many local materials, it radiates the warmth and spirit of the craftsmen who built it.

Grandview Residence, California, 1996: A sweeping entry wall with deep-set windows embraces the home and continues inside, setting up key elements that articulate the interior spaces. Colors are layered to define forms and materials. Steel curls, glass waves, stone floats, and wood shimmers in luminous tones.

Forest View Residence, California, 1994: Rhythms of windows and columns add order to this design; spaces flow into and through each other, open yet divided by shape, texture, and color. The warped plane of the ceiling directs sunlight into a central courtyard; windows in the circular shower capture light from sunrise to sunset.

Private Residence, California, 1988: Palladian proportions, classic symmetry, and axiality give order to the sculpted and serene spaces of this villa. Living spaces spill onto sun-drenched terraces and gardens; light and shadow playing on thick walls provides a sense of solidity and permanence.

[Left] **A House for Two Architects, San Miguel de Allende, Mexico:** 1 Courtyard with the kitchen and outdoor dining area; 2 Detail at the master bedroom cabinet; 3 View of the stair from entry; 4 Stairway. Photo credit: Steven House

[Below] **Grandview Residence, California:** 1 Detail of the openings at the front wall; 2 Detail of shelving in the library; 3 Stair at the entrance. Photo credit: Steven House

[Above] **Forest View Residence, California:** 1 Rear facade; 2 View of the master bedroom and stair railing; 3 Dining room; 4 Master shower. Photo credits: courtesy *House Beautiful*; Christopher Irion [1–4]

[Right] **Private Residence, California:** 1 Rear facade from the pool; 2 View of the living room from the entrance. Photo credit: Gerald Ratto

Eva Jiricna
United Kingdom

"True freedom is to try with each successive project to do something different and better. To try to interpret an old principle in a new way, to do better tomorrow on what missed the target today."

PROFESSIONAL HISTORY AND FIRM PROFILE

Eva Jiricna graduated as an architect/engineer from the University of Prague in 1962. In 1968 she was hired by the Greater London Council in London, and was still abroad when the Russians invaded Czechoslovakia later that year. She was not to return for more than twenty years. In 1969, she began working with the Louis de Soissons Partnership on the Brighton Marina project, eventually becoming project architect.

In 1978, Jiricna founded Jiricna Hodges; her first solo project was a small retail outlet for Joseph Ettedgui. In 1980, she designed the interior for Le Caprice restaurant in London, again for Ettedgui, which has remained unchanged and is still cited for design excellence. In 1984, she was employed by Richard Rogers Partnership to design interior packages for the Lloyds Headquarters Building in London, including the Captain's Room restaurant (no longer existing) and specific features such as the underwriters' desks and lighting units.

In 1985, Jiricna formed Eva Jiricna Architects in London. Throughout the 1980s and 1990s, the practice completed retail, restaurant, residential, and commercial projects for clients including Harrod's, Joseph Ltd., Joan & David (more than fifty outlets worldwide), and Hugo Boss, and became widely known for innovative work using glass and steel, notably staircases in retail, leisure, and residential sites.

In 1989, after the "Velvet Revolution" in Prague, Jiricna was finally able to travel to the Czech Republic. She was appointed architectural consultant by President Vaçlav Havel in 1995, and was commissioned to rebuild a new orangery on the site of the fifteenth-century original at Prague Castle. That same year she was commissioned by Andersen Consulting to do the interiors of its Czech headquarters, in the Rasin Building designed by Frank Gehry. Throughout 1996 and 1997, the firm completed interiors for Andersen's other Eastern European offices. Projects have also included a new library extension for De Montfort University in Leicester, England (1994); the Canada Water Bus Station in London (1995); and the Faith Zone for the Millennium Dome exhibition in Greenwich, London (1999). Recent commissions include interiors for prestigious jewelers Boodle & Dunthorne at sites in and out of London; "Marcus" on Bond Street for Time Products (also jewelers), London; the new Hotel Rybna in central Prague; and Amec plc, one of the UK's largest commercial corporations.

Jiricna has been a council member for the Architectural Association (AA), Royal Institute of British Architects (RIBA), and Royal Academy of Arts. She teaches at the Academy of Applied Arts in Prague, and has received honorary doctorates from the University of Southampton (UK) and the University of Brno (Czech Republic). She is sought after as a lecturer, symposium leader, critic, and jury member by academic and professional organizations worldwide.

Selected Awards

Interiors Magazine Retail Award, 1999, 1995, 1991, 1990

Academician, Royal Academy of Arts, 1996

Fellow, Royal Society of Arts, 1996

CBE (Commander of the British Empire) for services to Interior Design, 1994

Design prize, Royal Academy of Arts, London, summer staircase exhibition, 1994

Selected Publications

Jiricna, Eva. *Staircases*. New York: Watson-Guptill Publications, 2001.

McGuire, Penny. "Fragile State: Orangery at Prague Castle." *Architectural Review*, January 2000.

McGuire, Penny. "Quay Signature: Canada Water Bus Station, London." *Architectural Review*, June 2000.

Zevon, Susan. "Czech Tech." *House Beautiful*, December 1999.

Greenberg, Stephen. "Reading between the Lines: Eva Jiricna Architect's University Library, Leicester." *RIBA Journal*, December 1998.

Selected Clients

[Clients based in the UK unless otherwise noted.]

Amec plc

Andersen Consulting, *East European offices*

De Montfort University

Jubilee Line Extension

Prague Castle, *Prague, Czech Republic*

Stadtkrug Hotel & Restaurants, *Prague, Czech Republic*

DESIGN STATEMENT

The greatest challenge is to create architecture that enriches our life experience.

A given architectural concept is open to as many interpretations and variations as there are architects. No longer is it necessary for the architect to know how a visualized structure might work—the level of existing technologies is such that experts can build more or less anything that has been drawn. The palette of architectural styles has widened, and excellence and professional competence can be found anywhere, no matter which of the different architectural philosophies an architect or group espouses.

I am still drawn to ever-inspiring possibilities of structural systems and methods. Nothing gives me greater pleasure than combining a selected design concept with the most suitable method of construction, choosing materials for their inherent qualities, integrating both sides of the coin to create one simple, clean, visually pleasing harmony. One can look at nature itself for a similar pattern: On the one hand, nature displays an endless variety of shapes and forms, a seemingly limitless imagination; on the other, the possibilities are shaped by an obedience to the law of gravity. Each cell in our body carries in its memory the process of nature's creation, from day one to the present. This creative process is ever-present in our subconscious, and is perhaps also subconsciously present in our judgment of a designed object, enriching the intellectual and creative process of any design.

Architecture is no longer a discipline in which a designer/architect is responsible for the entire result: Teams of experts participate in the design process. But there are still those who make it happen, who transmit enthusiasm, who lead, who point everyone in the same direction. The abilities to communicate the aim and to control the skills are qualities that I not only consider virtues, but that I also enjoy.

That little word "enjoy" is crucial. Architecture should be creative, knowledgeable, professional, and imaginative. But whatever adjectives one might use, it has to above all be fun, and ought to enrich our life experience in the most enjoyable manner possible.

ILLUSTRATED PROJECTS

Canada Water Bus Station, Jubilee Line Extension, London, 1999

Joan & David, Paris, 1994

Orangery, Prague Castle, Prague, Czech Republic, 1996

Private Residence, Knightsbridge, London, 1992

Joe's Café, London, 1988

Private Apartment, Prague, Czech Republic, 1998

Ove Arup House, Highgate, UK, 1993

[Below] **Canada Water Bus Station, London:** View of entrance, with aero-foil projection roof that muffles sound for nearby apartments, protects passengers below from inclement weather, and deflects nighttime illumination.
Photo credit: Richard Bryant

[Below] **Joan & David, Paris:** 1&2 Views of glass and stainless steel staircase, designed to have minimal impact while providing a transparent connection between two floors of retail space. The stairway is suspended by a series of rods and central stainless steel mesh.
Photo credit: Katsuhisa Kida

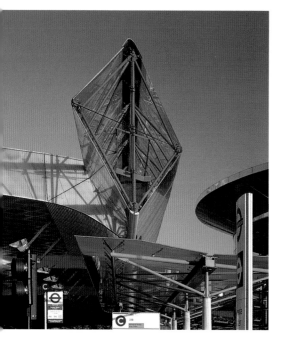

Orangery, Prague Castle, Prague, Czech Republic:
1 Exterior view of steel and glass structure, with castle in background; 2 Interior view with orange trees and fountain in midground. Photo credit: Richard Bryant

124

[Left] **Private residence, Knightsbridge, London:** View looking down glass and stainless steel staircase, an attempt to interpret a 19th-century English interior in late-20th-century vernacular. Individual glass treads, suspended from a beam of steel mesh, are sandblasted with a diamond pattern for a non-slip finish and to achieve a decorative effect on the basement floor. Photo credit: Richard Bryant/Arcaid

[Below] **Joe's Café, London:** A "wraparound" wall conceals drainage pipes and breaks up the small space's severe geometry. Stainless steel cable serves as lightweight balustrading to divide the space. Photo credit: Alistair Hunter

[Above] **Private Apartment, Prague, Czech Republic:** 1 Interior view along corridor past kitchen; 2 View of staircase with sunlight. Photo credit: Richard Bryant

[Above] **Ove Arup House, Highgate, London:** 1 View of extension over new swimming pool, with enclosure and privacy provided by a variety of glazed screens; 2 View through new extension. Photo credit: Richard Bryant

Sulan Kolatan
United States of America

"How can 'the house' participate in the emerging paradigms, technologies, ecologies, and economies that are shaping this new millennium and at the same time provide security and comfort, and a sense of belonging, for its occupants?"

PROFESSIONAL HISTORY

Sulan Kolatan was educated in Turkey and Germany. She divided her time between these two countries until 1983, when she received an Engineering Diploma from Rheinisch-Westfalische Technische Hochschule, Aachen, Germany. A year later she was awarded a scholarship and moved to New York to attend Columbia University, from which she graduated with a master's degree in science and building design.

Kolatan continues to maintain professional and academic ties to both Germany and Turkey. She has lectured in Berlin and Frankfurt; her work has been exhibited at the Deutsches Architekturmuseum in Frankfurt, featured on German television, and published in a number of German publications. As part of the Architektursommer 2000 in Hamburg, there was a profile on her together with an exhibition of her work in the show entitled "Women and Xtended Visions." In 1993 and 1995, Kolatan conducted workshops in Istanbul, which were focused on urban issues of the late twentieth century. In 1996, she presented the resulting material, together with a proposal for new urban strategies, at the second International HABITAT Conference on Cities in Istanbul.

Before founding Kolatan/MacDonald Studio in 1988, Kolatan acquired extensive professional experience in designing projects of significant scale, first in collaboration with Oswald Mathias Ungers, and later as a senior designer at Kohn Pedersen Fox Associates.

In addition to her practice, she has taught architecture at Columbia University's Graduate School of Architecture, Planning, and Preservation since 1990. Kolatan lectures, teaches, and attends design conferences internationally. She lives in New York City.

Selected Awards

American Institute of Architects Citation Award, Project Category, 1999

Nomination, International Media & Architecture Biennial, Graz, Austria

44th Annual Progressive Architecture Citation Award, 1997

New York Foundation for the Arts Grant and Fellowship, 1997

40 Under 40 (North America), 1995

Emerging Voices Competition, 1992

Selected Publications

Kol/Mac. Monograph. New York: Princeton Architectural Press (due 2001).

"After 2000." *Domus Magazine*, issue 822, Milan, January 2000.

Brayer, Marie Ange and Frederick Migayrou (eds.). *Archilab Orleans 2000*. Ville d'Orleans: FRAC, 2000.

GA Houses "Project 1999." *Global Architecture*, Tokyo, 1999.

Salazar, Jaime and Manuel Gausa (eds.). *Singular Housing*. Barcelona: Actar, 1999.

Zellner, Peter (ed.). *Hybrid Space: New Forms in Digital Architecture*. London: Thames & Hudson/New York: Rizzoli, 1999.

"The Shape of Things to Come," *The New York Times* Inaugural Color Issue, 1997.

FIRM PROFILE

Since its inception, Kolatan/MacDonald Studio has operated as a "lateral practice." As such, it has produced a series of projects of widely varying scale and context, with each one addressing specific issues concerning contemporary design culture. Sulan Kolatan and her partner, Bill MacDonald, have sought to expand the firm's scope to include architectural interiors, buildings, urban design, installations, Worldwide Web projects, product design, and competitions. In doing so, they have been able to pursue theoretical and experimental projects, and practice at the same time. Their client base is varied, and includes individual home-owners, commercial clients, and cultural and academic institutions. The concept of a lateral practice allows Kolatan and MacDonald to keep the boundaries of their practice fluid, and they are able to engage categories at once in a single project; for example, the Angelika Film Center project included architecture, furniture, equipment, and Web site design.

The work of Kolatan/MacDonald Studio is in the permanent collection of the Museum of Modern Art, as well as at other prominent institutions with international reputations. In 1999, their work was included in the "Housings" exhibition at Artist's Space in New York; in the "Un-Private House" exhibition at the Museum of Modern Art in New York; and in the international exhibition entitled "HOME, the twentieth century house," part of "Glasgow 1999—UK City of Architecture and Design," held in Glasgow, Scotland. The studio participated in shows in Germany and Italy in the fall of 1999, and in the first Design Triennial held at the Cooper Hewitt National Design Museum in New York City in March 2000.

DESIGN STATEMENT

The most challenging project is, by definition, always the one currently being worked on.

Within the larger framework of the design research of Kolatan/MacDonald Studio, each project provokes a new set of investigations. The overall direction of the research is therefore negotiated between already established, general parameters of interest fully within the studio's control and particular issues brought into play by accident with each project. One of the projects the practice is currently working on, "Housings," began in the spring of 1999 as an installation at Artist's Space in New York City and is now being developed into an extended research project on the range of contemporary modes of living and new prefabrication techniques. The project's primary challenge derives from this question: How can the house participate in the new paradigms, theories, technologies, ecologies, and economies shaping this new millennium while also providing security, comfort, and a sense of belonging for its occupants?

The house is perhaps one of the most difficult architectural problems in that it constitutes the most private of realms. The "home" is both a physical and a psychological territory for its owners. Kolatan/MacDonald Studio is interested in addressing the notion of "home" and its internal resistance to change by simultaneously investigating two strong forces of change in design culture today: the introduction of the computer as a quasi-intelligent tool in architectural design, and new digital production techniques in manufacturing. The response to the question posed above will have to be derived from this apparent paradox.

ILLUSTRATED PROJECTS

Yokohama International Port Terminal, Yokohama, Japan, 1995

O/K Apartment, New York City, 1996

Angelika Film Center, New York City, 1995

Moot Court, Southern New England School of Law, North Dartmouth, Massachusetts, 1997

Take 5 on Manhattan, New York City, 1997

Vehicles, digital images, 1996

Raybould House and Garden, Connecticut, 1997–present

Yokohama International Port Terminal, Yokohama, Japan: 1 Computer model. Perspective view toward the drop-off area visible in the distance. The multi-story departure hall appears in the foreground, its open volume produced by a thinning of the top layer into a roof membrane; 2 Overall view of the computer model showing all three program layers in different colors. The layers move through each other, mixing and connecting various programs; 3 Computer model. Plan view of departure level with program layers such as the drop-off and parking areas showing through. Holes in the layers represent vertical transitions throughout the building. Photo credit: courtesy Kolatan/MacDonald Studio

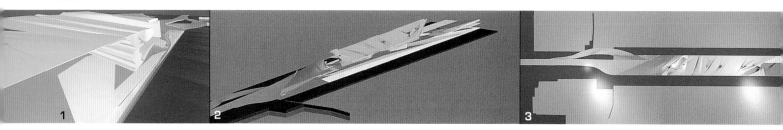

[Above] **O/K Apartment, New York City:**
1 Interior view of loft space with pivoting concrete table and concrete countertop; 2 Interior view with cement-board pivoting/ sliding partitions that connect or divide the space; 3 Interior view of master bedroom, with bathroom seen through the sliding glass partition. The aluminum laminated plywood wardrobe transforms into a vanity and built-in stainless-steel sink; 4 Detail view of continuous modified acrylic resin molded surface in master bedroom. A clear glass partition keeps the bathtub water back while providing a visual connection. Photo credit: Michael Moran

[Right] **Angelika Film Center, New York City:** 1 Computer models of new lobby furniture recombinations before they are "grounded" by columns in the lobby; 2 View of Angelika Film Center lobby, with one of the new furniture pieces wrapped around an existing column. A cinephile is shown previewing a film through a handheld personal monitor while operating a camera in one of the film theaters via remote control. Some of the film-images viewed are periodically uploaded onto a Web site designed as an extension of the lobby, both in terms of aesthetics and resources. Photo credit: courtesy Kolatan/MacDonald Studio

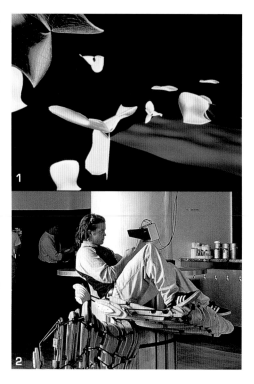

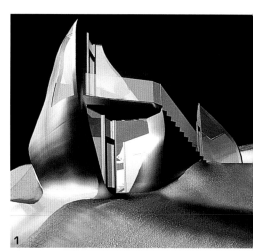

[Below] **Moot Court, Southern New England School of Law, North Dartmouth, Massachusetts:** Computer model of court interior with "inner lining" consisting of continuous media wall and ceiling with perforations for audio/visual equipment and light. Photo credit: courtesy Kolatan/MacDonald Studio

[Below] **Take 5 on Manhattan, New York City:** 1 Collage of aerial photograph of Midtown Manhattan with computer models of proposed rooftop structures. The projected programs include expanded office space mixed with recreational open-air space for the public; 2 Computer model of recreational open-air space inside a proposed structure; 3 Collage of aerial photograph of Harlem with computer model of proposed street-level structure. Projected program is a commercial space mixed with recreational open-air space for the public. Photo credit: courtesy Kolatan/MacDonald Studio

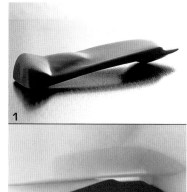

[Above] **Vehicles, digital images:** 1 Fiberglass model of 9-inch vehicle. One of six experimental designs for a new product series; 2 Computer model of interior of vehicle shown above. Photo credit: courtesy Kolatan/MacDonald Studio

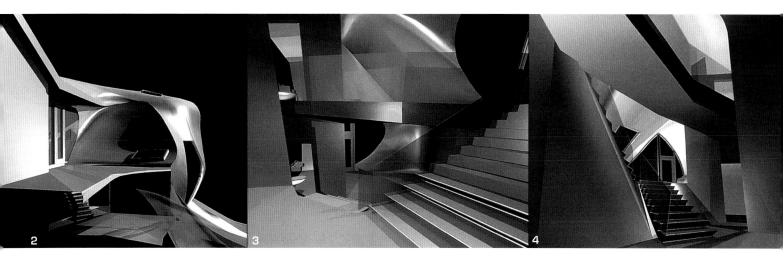

[Above] **Raybould House and Garden, Connecticut:** 1 Computer model. Exterior view of monocoque shell from lower garden, with stair connecting the upper bedroom to the garden; 2 Exterior view from entrance deck with existing saltbox house in front and new addition in back; 3 Interior perspective from upper sitting area toward lower sitting area, with stair to entrance hall on the right; 4 Interior perspective from lower sitting area toward upper sitting area, with bridge to upper bedroom overhead. Photo credit: courtesy Kolatan/MacDonald Studio

Eve Laron
Australia

*"The male culture that dominates architecture will not change
until 40 to 50 percent of practicing architects are women."*

PROFESSIONAL HISTORY

Eve Laron studied architecture and solar design at Technion, Israel Institute of Technology, Haifa, in the 1950s, and at the same time practiced as a student with several architectural firms in Israel. In 1955 she came to Sydney, Australia, and over the next two decades worked with a number of different architectural practices, designing and documenting a variety of building types.

In 1965 Laron was registered by the Board of Architects of New South Wales and in 1966 she was elected associate of the Royal Australian Institute of Architects. In the early 1970s, she became a partner in Eric Towell and Partners, Architects, specializing as a design architect for luxury high-rise home units and townhouse developments. In 1975 she was elected fellow of the Royal Australian Institute of Architects and in 1975 an associate of the Royal Institute of British Architects.

Laron was awarded a bachelor of arts in behavioral science at Macquarie University, Sydney, in 1979, and the same year was presented with an award for Excellence in Housing for Environmental Design. In 1984 she established her own practice, Eve Laron Architects. The firm quickly established a reputation for design excellence, and in 1989–1990, Laron's work was a featured exhibition at the University of Adelaide library.

Throughout her career, in addition to her work as a designer and architect Laron has participated in various related activities. In 1983, she founded Constructive Women, Inc., the Association of Women Architects, Landscape Architects, Planners, Engineers, and Women in the Building Industry. In 1988, she presented the Women in the Arts seminar of the Federation of Business and Professional Women, New South Wales, Australia, and in 1991 was a representative for the Royal Australian Institute of Architects on the New South Wales Pool Fence Legislation Review Committee. Since 1991 she has been a member of the Advisory Committee on Environmental Policy for the Royal Australian Institute of Architects. Currently she holds regular seminars on solar and environmental design at the Sydney Building Information Centre and makes frequent guest appearances on Australian commercial television to speak on solar and environmental designs.

Selected Publications

Hollo, Nick. "'Warm House, Cool House': Inspirational Designs for Low-Energy Housing." *Choice*, Australian Consumer's Association, 1995.

Master, Margaret. "25 Great Home Renovations." *Nationwide News*, 1993.

Lorenz, Clare. *Women in Architecture*. London: Trefoil, 1990.

FIRM PROFILE

Eve Laron Architects, based in Killara, New South Wales, Australia, was established in 1980. The firm specializes in alterations and small-scale residential developments, and to date has designed over 200 houses and alterations. Laron has long been a passionate and articulate advocate of solar and environmental design, to which she brings a decidedly commonsensical approach. In a 1992 radio talk show on passive solar energy, Laron said, "Contrary to popular belief, 'solar design' doesn't mean any particular visual style. It certainly doesn't mean something weird and metallic-looking, as some people seem to image. The Alhambra in Spain is good solar design—so is the igloo of an eskimo—and hundreds of styles in between." Eve Laron Architects definitely practices what Laron preaches, and has designed an extraordinary variety of environmentally sound residences that are also quite beautiful.

DESIGN STATEMENT

All design is challenging, and your next project is always the best.

Eve Laron finds that the more challenging a project—that is, the more difficulties it entails—the more interesting the solution. In the very act of resolving a given problem, one usually introduces some quite fascinating details that one would not have come up with were it not for the pressure to overcome that problem. Necessity is, indeed, not only the mother of invention, but also the mother of inspiration.

ILLUSTRATED PROJECTS

Malouf Residence, digital image

Passive Solar House, Lindfield, NSW, Australia, 1992

Private Residence, Balgowlah, NSW, Australia, 1995

Private Residence, Turramurra, NSW, Australia, 1989

Renovated House, Killara, NSW, Australia, 1985

Lee House, digital image

Private Residence, Taree, NSW, Australia, 1985

Riverview Renovation, Riverview, NSW, Australia, 1995

(Above) **Malouf Residence:** Photo credit: courtesy Eve Laron Architects

(Below) **Private Residence, Balgowlah, NSW, Australia:** 1 Diagonal design allows the northern sun and eastern view to enter every room; 2 "Cut-out" in the brick wall allows light into the hallway. Photo credit: courtesy Eve Laron Architects

(Above) **Passive Solar House, Lindfield, NSW, Australia:** 1 Northwest façade showing glazed veranda with shade cloth cover; 2 North elevation.
Photo credit: courtesy Eve Laron Architects

(Above) **Private Residence, Turramurra, NSW, Australia:** 1 External view of the screened veranda; 2 Living areas open onto sun-filled northern terraces; 3 Glazed screened verandah.
Photo credit: courtesy Eve Laron Architects

(Above) **Renovated House, Killara, NSW, Australia:**
A screened solarium, shaded in summer.
Photo credit: courtesy Eve Laron Architects

(Below) **Lee House:** Photo credit: courtesy Eve Laron Architects

(Below) **Private Residence, Taree, NSW, Australia:** 1 View of the kitchen, opening to the dining room and screened veranda; 2 Open rosewood stair in the circular sandstone brick stairwell. Photo credit: courtesy Eve Laron Architects

(Above) **Riverview Renovation, Riverview, NSW, Australia:** 1 Sky dome gives light to living areas and shade cloth prevents heat from entering in midsummer; 2 Bathroom has glazed wall and ceiling surrounded by rocky garden; 3 New skylight lights up formerly dark kitchen. Photo credit: courtesy Eve Laron Architects

MJ Long
United Kingdom

"Appropriately, this photograph of me with my husband, Sir Colin St. John Wilson, was taken in the entrance hall of London's new British Library, which we designed together and which was recently voted one of the ten best-loved buildings of the millennium by a popular poll in London."

PROFESSIONAL HISTORY

In 1960, MJ Long was awarded a bachelor of arts degree from Smith College in Northampton, Massachusetts, where she graduated with distinction. In 1964 she received a master's of architecture from Yale University, and the same year she was awarded the Paris Prize, a national architectural thesis competition.

In 1965, Long moved to England and joined the office of Colin St. John Wilson; she was made a partner in 1972. More than half of Long's time with the firm was spent as co-designer of the British Library, which was completed in 1994. Long also did a succession of studios for well-known London artists. Upon completion of the British Library, she co-founded Long & Kentish, Architects with Rolfe Kentish, an associate from the British Library project.

Long has taught a design studio and supporting seminar courses at the Yale School of Architecture every year since 1973. She has also taught in England, is a member of the Royal Institute of British Architects (RIBA) Visiting Board, and has held three- to five-year appointments as an external examiner at six British schools of architecture. In 1995 she was elected "Brother" of the London Art Workers' Guild; in 1996 she was appointed to the Architectural Advisory Panel of the Heritage Lottery Fund in the United Kingdom; and in 1997 she joined the Editorial Board of *Architectural Review Quarterly*, a refereed journal published in London. She has been an invited speaker at venues throughout the United States and the United Kingdom, and is a member of the RIBA and the American Institute of Architects (AIA).

Selected Awards

Grand Award for Architecture, Royal Academy Summer Exhibition, for gallery in Chichester (England), 2000

Award for Design Excellence, Standing Conference on National and University Libraries, for the Queen Mary College Library, 1988

Selected Publications

Hellen, Nicholas. "Andrew Liberates Nation's Sea Treasures." *The Sunday Times* (London), 30 July 2000.

Blundell-Jones, Peter. "Speaking Volumes." *The Architectural Review*, June 1998.

Bevan, Robert. "Perspective: Long & Kentish." *Building Design*, 5 April 1996.

FIRM PROFILE

Although the partnership of Long & Kentish, Architects was established less than a decade ago, both partners have been architects for more than thirty years, enabling the practice to offer both new energy and extensive experience. The number of architects at the firm varies according to workload, resulting in the strengths of a large office and the flexibility of response of a smaller one.

Because of both partners' extensive work on the British Library, many of the firm's projects have been related to library design. Its second academic library for Brighton University is now under construction, as is an extension to the public library in Newport, Rhode Island (done in association with Hammond Beeby Rupert Ainge of Chicago). Long and Kentish have acted as library design consultants for the National Art Library, the European Parliament Library, and the National Library of Singapore.

The firm's two largest current commissions are for the National Maritime Museum Cornwall, in Falmouth, Cornwall, UK, and a new gallery extension for Pallant House Gallery in Chichester, UK (in association with Colin St. John Wilson).

Another recurring type of commission is for artist's studios; at least one has been under construction since the firm was founded. Throughout its history, much of the firm's work has involved restoration work or historic environments.

DESIGN STATEMENT

We see design as a process of discovery, in which the form of the building gradually evolves from recognition of what it is and what it does.

We do not start with what the building looks like, but with an appropriate anatomy for its structures and spaces. The appropriateness of the result is more important to us than the fact that it is recognized as one of ours. As a result, our buildings are different in appearance from each other in ways that are analogous to the differences between their locations and their occupants.

The Aldrich Library for the University of Brighton was won in competition in 1994 and opened in 1996. Its site is at the northern extremity of a succession of buildings, most dating from the 1960s. The shape of the building was designed to give all readers good views of the downs to the north, and to buffer the library's collections from the southern sun. The

very low-budget building is naturally ventilated, with air intakes along a light shelf; it is also acoustically buffered to eliminate traffic noise from outside. All readers are given electrical and data ports and individual desk lights, all of which are fed from the perimeter of the shallow section building. Materials are natural, with wood used for doors and furniture. Secondary skins (suspended ceilings and gyproc walls) are kept to a minimum. The library's angled facade turns the corner, which marks the extremity of the campus. Materials and colors are generally related to its bulky 1960s neighbors, but articulated detail makes it "special" and helps to announce its role as a focus for academic activity in spite of its small size.

A second project, the Falmouth Maritime Museum, was started in 1996 and is now under construction, to be opened in phases between September 2001 and June 2002. The project is located at the heart of the waterfront in Falmouth, Cornwall—between the historic town on one side and large commercial docks on the other—and includes shops, restaurants, offices, a multiplex cinema, a marina, and an "events square." But the jewel in the crown is the National Maritime Museum Cornwall, a 45,000-square-foot building that will house the 120 small boats belonging to the National Maritime Museum in Greenwich, together with a local maritime collection.

As much about wind and water as about the boats themselves, the museum will have a tower overlooking the navigational marks of the harbor, a tidal gallery that will be entirely underwater at high tide, and a tidal pool to bring boats on the water into the museum. The client's wish for a landmark building has been satisfied through the general massing and location of the buildings, but the materials and colors are purposely retiring—predominantly the silver-gray of weathered oak, slate, and granite, which are typical of the area and will work as a backdrop to flags, sails, awnings, and banners. A tradition of building language is thus recalled, although the specific spatial and constructional detailing is entirely modern.

ILLUSTRATED PROJECTS

Falmouth Maritime, National Maritime Museum, Cornwall, UK, slated for completion in 2002

Aldrich Library, University of Brighton, Brighton, UK, 1996

Aldrich Library, University of Brighton, Brighton, UK: 1 Floor plans. Left: ground floor with computer suites; right: plan typical of the three upper floors, with readers along window walls; 2&3 Window-cleaning walkways, which also act as sunscreens; louvers in the facade are fresh-air intakes; 4 View out to trees and south downs; 5 Exterior view from the north; 6 Reader tables, with perimeter electrical and data distribution. Light shelf above also acts as acoustic baffle for fresh air; 7 Stairway, which participates in the light and airy atmosphere. Photo credits: courtesy of Long & Kentish, Architects [2]; Bob Seago [6]; MJ Long [4, 7]; Duncan McNeill [3, 5]

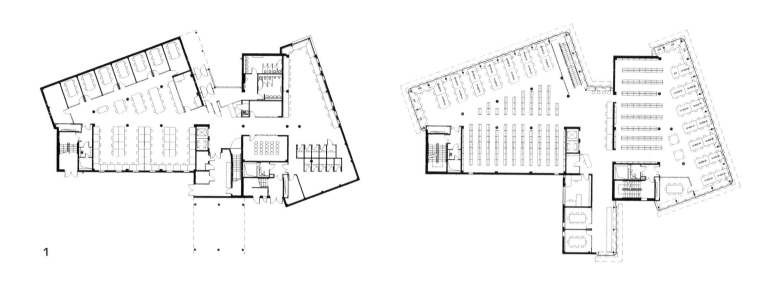

Falmouth Maritime, National Maritime Museum, Cornwall, UK: 1 Sketch of waterfront showing proposed museum (center) and events square (right). The new buildings are distributed so as to bridge the scale difference between the docks to the left and the town to the right; 2 Photomontage of waterfront; 3 Site model. The museum's facade will also act as stage house for performances in the new square; 4 Study model, showing the tower and next to it the tidal pool and pontoon; 5 Exhibition model demonstrating boat collection sailing through a daylit gallery; 6 Site plan, with north at the top. Spaces outside the museum are varied to offer glimpses of the water as well as wide views. There are protected south-facing sun traps for winter. Photo credits: coutesy of MJ Long [1, 3]; Long & Kentish, Architects [2, 4, 5]

1

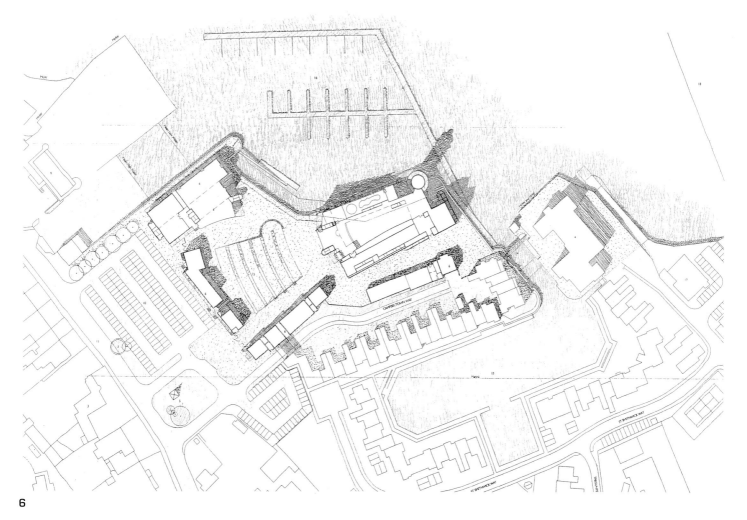

6

Victoria Meyers
United States of America

"The more we build, the more our source of inspiration comes from nature and, more specifically, from light. The creation of space in architecture is the condensation and purification of the power of light. Light makes the relationships that bind human beings and nature. It is this vital relationship between light and the forces of nature, interpreted through the eyes of a modern mind searching for spaces relevant to the twenty-first century, which inspires my work."

PROFESSIONAL HISTORY

Victoria Meyers attended Lafayette College in Pennsylvania, receiving a joint bachelor's degree in art history and civil engineering in 1978. In 1982, she was awarded a master's in architecture from Harvard University's Graduate School of Design. Meyers's broad, cross-disciplinary background has been an influence on her architectural work; her design aesthetic reaches beyond architecture to reference other arts as well as mathematical theory. After graduating, Meyers spent two years in the office of British architect Richard Rogers, where she produced working drawings and supervised construction for the only Rogers building in the United States, the PaTSCenter in Princeton, New Jersey. The project exposed her to the use and detailing of steel, glass, and concrete—materials she continues to use in her work.

In 1985, Meyers and Tom Hanrahan co-founded Hanrahan + Meyers Architects in New York City. As design principal, Meyers works closely with clients, especially in the detailing of projects. Among her many projects over the years is the Holley Loft, completed in 1995 in New York City, a residential project that revolved around an exploration of the ambiguities between inside and outside. Light penetrates deep into the apartment from windows facing Broadway, while movable panels allow the creation of smaller, more intimate spaces for guests. The materials used—wood, stone, steel, glass—resulted in a truly exquisite space. The Holley Loft has been featured on two book covers, in a show at the Museum of Modern Art (MoMA) in 1999, in several national and international publications, and on CNN.

Meyers also organizes the design and fabrication of custom lighting and furnishings, allowing her to move from the macro scale of urban design to the micro scale of the human body. Three of her designs—an umbrella stand, an occasional table, and a magazine rack—are in the permanent collection of the MoMA Design Store.

Meyers is an active member of the Architectural League of New York, the American Institute of Architects (AIA), the Van Alen Institute, and the Lafayette College Leadership Council, as well as a fellow of the Institute for Urban Design. She is also a participant and former mentor in the Women's International House Leadership Program and serves as the coordinator and a part-time instructor for Advanced Design Studies at the Columbia University Graduate School.

Selected Awards

AIA Design Award, 1998, 1997, 1996, 1991, 1990, 1989

AIA Design Citation, 1995, 1993, 1992, 1989

Architectural Record Interiors Award, 1995

40 Under 40, 1995

Graham Foundation Grant, 1994

New York Foundation for the Arts, Artist's Fellow, 1994

Architectural League of New York, Emerging Voices Award, 1993

Council for the Arts, Massachusetts Institute of Technology, Eugene McDermott Award, 1993

Selected Publications

Meyers, V. *Geometry and Experience.* Brooklyn, New York: Pierogi Press, 1999. (Available through the Pieriogi Gallery in Brooklyn.)

Meyers, V. "Space and the Perception of Time." *Journal of Architectural Education*, November 1999.

Ojeda, Oscar Riera, ed. *The New American Apartment.* New York: Watson-Guptill Publications, 1997.

Betsky, Aaron. 581 *Architects in the World.* Japan: TOTO Shuppan, 1995.

"Recent Work" [20-page retrospective of four projects]. *Architecture + Urbanism*, July 1992.

Meyers, Victoria. *House for Artists.* New York: V. Meyers, 1986.

FIRM PROFILE

Founded by Thomas Hanrahan and Victoria Meyers in 1985, Hanrahan + Meyers Architects has a diverse project list that includes housing; community, fine arts, and music performance centers; galleries; and university facilities.

In 1993, Hanrahan + Meyers was awarded the commission for the headquarters of AIA's New York chapter after submitting the winning design in a limited competition. In 1995, the firm's design for a new residential loft (the Holley Loft) in Manhattan received wide attention from the press, including articles in *Harper's Bazaar* and *Architectural Record*. Current projects include two community art centers for the New York City Housing Authority and a master plan study for the Battery Park City Authority.

In recent years, the firm has become increasingly involved with investigations of ideas such as transparency, invisibility, and weightlessness and how they are applied to actual buildings. Its most recent built work, the Red Hook Public Arts Center in Brooklyn, New York (see page 140), is the first in a new direction of investigating the "color of light," with light and color treated as material substances, just as wood, steel, or glass.

Selected Clients

Amano Corporate Headquarters

AIA, New York Chapter

Arts International

Battery Park City Authority

Columbia University

New York Academy of Art

New York City Housing Authority

Ojai Festival Performance Shell

Socrates Sculpture Park

DESIGN STATEMENT

The process of design requires a good client.

For Victoria Meyers, a "good" client is an integral part of the process—someone who gets behind you while you're designing and cheers you on.

Believe it or not, Meyers has had only good clients to this point. She attributes that to a conscious decision made some years ago, in 1990, to work only with clients who knew and appreciated her work. Meyers then spent two years showing potential clients the door and fretting that she would never work again. Then a funny thing happened: She started getting work. Today she only works with clients who support her and her talents.

Even if you have great clients, Meyers explains, the process of design is still a challenge. Architects, as artists, struggle to get everything as "right" and perfect as they can for their clients. Happily, this challenge is also a pleasure—each project is another vehicle for exploring the possibilities of expression, and the resulting success is very rewarding.

ILLUSTRATED PROJECTS

AIA, New York City Chapter, New York City, 1995

Duplicate House Model, Bedford, New York, 1998

Red Hook Public Arts Center, Brooklyn, New York, 1996–2000

Latimer Gardens Community Center, Queens, New York, 1998–current

MoMA Tower Apartments Renovation, New York City, 1998

[Opposite] **AIA, New York City Chapter:** 1 Reception area, with custom steel desk designed by architects; 2 Conference room, separated from public corridor by glass wall fitted with perforated aluminum panels; 3 View of entrance and its emphasis on a natural palette of modernist materials: wood, steel, and glass. Photo credit: Peter Aaron

[Below] **Duplicate House Model, Bedford, New York:** 1 View of house from garden. The house is read as a series of abstract planes and forms, with color helping to define the flow of space around planes; 2 View of house from car entrance, with two elevations reading as abstract planes and defining where the car enters the precinct of the house; 3 Elevation studies. A palette of plaster planes will hover above a landscape of glass, steel, and wood to define the various zones of the house. Materials become the defining element in an abstract landscape of color. Photo credit: Jock Pottle/ESTO

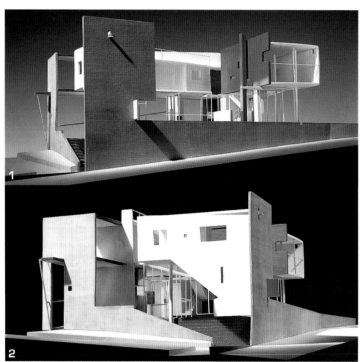

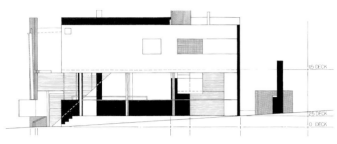

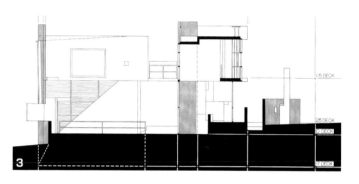

[Below] **Red Hook Public Arts Center, Brooklyn, New York:** 1 Exterior view. This facade emphasizes the importance of light and color, as well as materials; 2 View inside public art gallery. The use of color as a material saturates interior spaces with light and life; 3 View of red plane that marks the edge of public gallery. The plane sits next to a white wall awash in reflected red glow from a skylight; the play between planes with actual and reflected color animates the space; 4 View of inside/outside theater. The intense blue wall frames the view between theater and stage, and also gestures toward the public seating area to the south of the open rear proscenium. Photo credit: Arch Photo Eduard Hueber

1

2

3

Latimer Gardens Community Center, Queens, New York: 1 Computer model. The roof is a "wave" of energy that gently floats over and above new site, allowing existing landscape to flow beneath; 2 Side elevation adjacent to public walkway, with the roof "wave" hovering above the limestone wall; 3 Interior view, showing underside of roof "wave." The multipurpose space has a removable stage structure with stage lighting and sound system. Photo credit: Jock Pottle/ESTO

MoMA Tower Apartments Renovation, New York City: 1 View from bedroom looking toward entrance foyer. The play between reflective and matte surfaces creates a lively environment within a limited palette of natural materials (glass, stone, wood, and steel); 2 View into living area from entrance foyer. Curving glass above cherry cabinet emphasizes how spaces are connected through views, light, and materiality; 3 View into living area, with materials playing a dominant role in establishing a warm sensibility within the space; 4 Detail view of entrance door, with steel umbrella stand designed by Hanrahan + Meyers; 5 View from bath looking toward bedroom. Reflectivity, transparency, and beautiful materials are manipulated to create a deceptively large-seeming space; 6 Apartment plan. Photo credit: Peter Aaron/ESTO

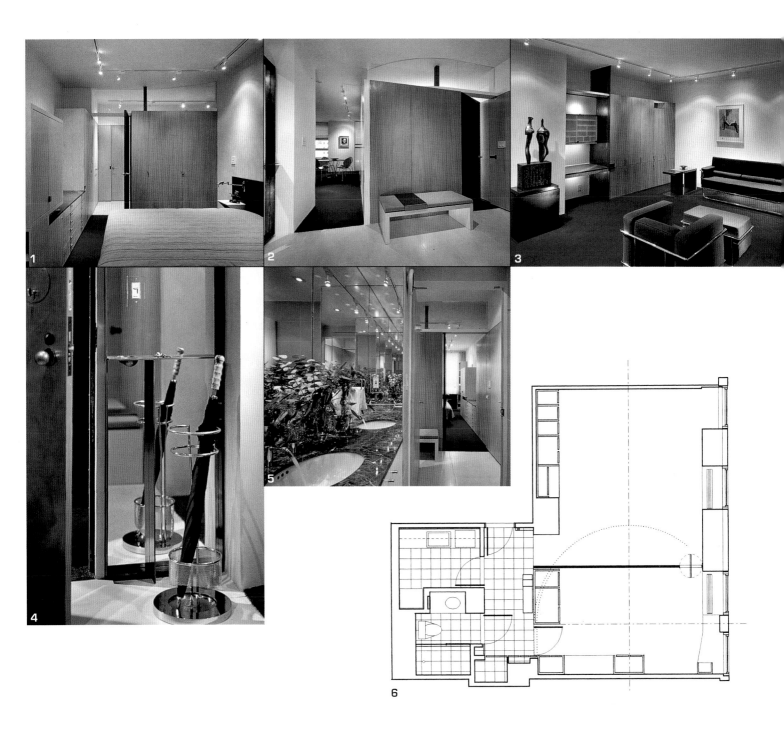

Carme Pinós
Spain

"The sensuality of the trace set down by the pencil in the hand, the material nature of a sheet of paper, the unfinished drawings sitting on the worktable—these all contribute to transforming the intangible to the tangible. They are the best way to reduce the distance between the architect and what is taking shape."

PROFESSIONAL HISTORY

Carme Pinós graduated from the School of Architecture, Barcelona, in 1979. In 1982, she established a partnership with Enric Miralles. From 1982 to 1991, the Pinós-Miralles partnership designed numerous projects that received critical acclaim, both in Spain and internationally, including the Igualada School and Cemetery Park and the Archery Ground for the Barcelona Olympic Games. In 1991 Carme Pinós established her own practice, Estudio Carme Pinós, and took charge of several projects begun while she and Miralles were partners, including the Hostalets de Balenya Civic Center, the La Mina Civic Center, and the Morella Boarding School.

Over the last decade, Pinós has combined her work as an architect with numerous teaching appointments, participation on competition juries, and lectures. She has been visiting professor in architecture at Urbana-Champaign, Illinois; the Academy Van Bouwkunst, Amsterdam; the Kunstakademie, Düsseldorf; L'Ecole Especiale D'Architecture, Paris; Escola Técnica Superior d'Arquitectura de Barcelona; Universidad Catolica, Chile; and Columbia University, New York. She has also given numerous lectures about her own work at various universities in Europe and America, such as Ecole Polytechnique Fédérale de Zürich; L'Ecole Especiale D'Architecture, Paris; the Universities of Darmstadt, Wuppertal, and Stuttgart, Germany; the Architectural League, Parsons School of Design, and Columbia University, New York; the University of Southern California-Los Angeles; and Harvard University.

Her recent work has been exhibited at the University of Stuttgart, the University of Illinois, the Gallery Architettura Arte Moderna of Rome, the Gallery Basic of Köln in Germany, the University La Sapienza in Rome, the Contemporary Art Museum of San Juan de Puerto Rico, and Architectuurcentrum AORTA in Utrecht.

Selected Awards

Dragados Award, Igualada Cemetery,1999

National Award of Architecture, Spain, 1995

FAD (Fomento de las Artes y del Diseñó) Prizes: La Mina Civic Center, Hostelets de Balenya Civic Center (1994), Igualada Cemetery, Olympic Archery Range (1991), "La Llauna" Factory remodeling (Interior Design Prize, 1987)

Barcelona City Award, Olympic Archery Range, 1992

Premier Bienal Arquitectura Española, La Llauna School, 1991

Selected Publications

"The Pedestrian Bridge at Petrer." *Casabella*, May 2000: 49–53.

"Women in Architecture and Construction." *Archicrée-Architecture Intérieure.* No. 291, 2000: 124–125.

"Abroad Perspective (Boarding School in Morella)." *California Architecture*, Summer 1999.

"Carme Pinós." *Architectural Review*, October 1999.

Slessor, Catherine. "Spanish Steps: Carme Pinós' Inventive Landscaping." *Architectural Review*, October 1999.

Carme Pinós: Selected Projects Since 1991. Monograph. Actar Publishing, Barcelona, 1999.

Ryan, Raymond, "Lyrical Geometry," *Architectural Review*, June 1996.

FIRM PROFILE

At Estudio Carme Pinós, which was established in 1991, Pinós and her colleagues seek coherence in the design process as a whole, from the first idea to the last on-site detail. The intention must be clear at any phase of a project.

From the beginning, the firm has begun the design process—those early moments of hunting for the idea, of defining the thought—with drawings, rather than models or computer simulations. The first models, which are always paper cutouts or bent wire, actually resemble drawings. The materials do not enclose spaces, but instead look like lines on the paper between which the spaces circulate in white. Use of the computer comes much later, when the design is clear.

The range of project types undertaken by Estudio Carme Pinós is evidence of the firm's versatility: landscape architecture, public housing, public parks, sports centers, civic centers, schools at all levels, commercial structures, private residences. They have designed projects for cemeteries and waterfronts, and one of their most well-known designs (illustrated on page 147) is a pedestrian bridge.

Recently, in addition to the projects illustrated here, Carme Pinós has designed a seaside promenade, Orihuela, Murcia; the Torrevieja Waterfront, Alicante; a secondary school in Mollerusa, Lleida; and a leisure center and landscaping arrangement at the pond of Caldas de Reis, Galicia.

DESIGN STATEMENT

The challenges of any project are met by the process.

The sensuality of the trace set down by the pencil in the hand, the material nature of a sheet of paper, the unfinished drawings sitting on the worktable, these all contribute to transforming the intangible to the tangible. They are the best way to reduce the distance between the architect and what is taking shape.

The firm avoids frontal views, preferring to seek the tangential. This approach is linked with its perception and understanding of space. Carme Pinós believes that we understand space in relation to motion: movements that rebound in space, that take the measure of space.

Spatial visions are overlapped: the building and what is behind it, the landscape, the building overall.

More than drawing plans, the firm illustrates experiences. Anything that speaks to it of life, helps it understand human behaviour, everyday human concerns and needs—anything that helps the firm to give tangible shape to those concerns commands its utmost attention.

ILLUSTRATED PROJECTS

Fairgrounds, Jorge Vergara Center, Guadalajara, Mexico, 1999–2000. The Fairgrounds is one of ten distinct sections of a 750-acre business, educational, and entertainment complex just outside Guadalajara, commissioned by millionaire Jorge Vergara. One of the firm's primary objectives was to create a space that could be enjoyed as a park when not being used as a fairgrounds.

Pedestrian Bridge, Petrer, Alicante, Spain, 1997–1998. The commission was to design a footbridge across a dried-up riverbed between Petrer and an adjacent rural area, which did not have its own public square. More than just a footbridge between two points, the completed structure defines and articulates the connection between village and suburb.

Parc de ses Estaciones, Palma de Mallorca, Mallorca, Spain, under construction. The design of this park, situated as a gateway between the old town and newer sections of the city, involved reconfiguring the landscape in order to create distinct zones, at different levels, offering different qualities and different "windows" to the surrounding facades.

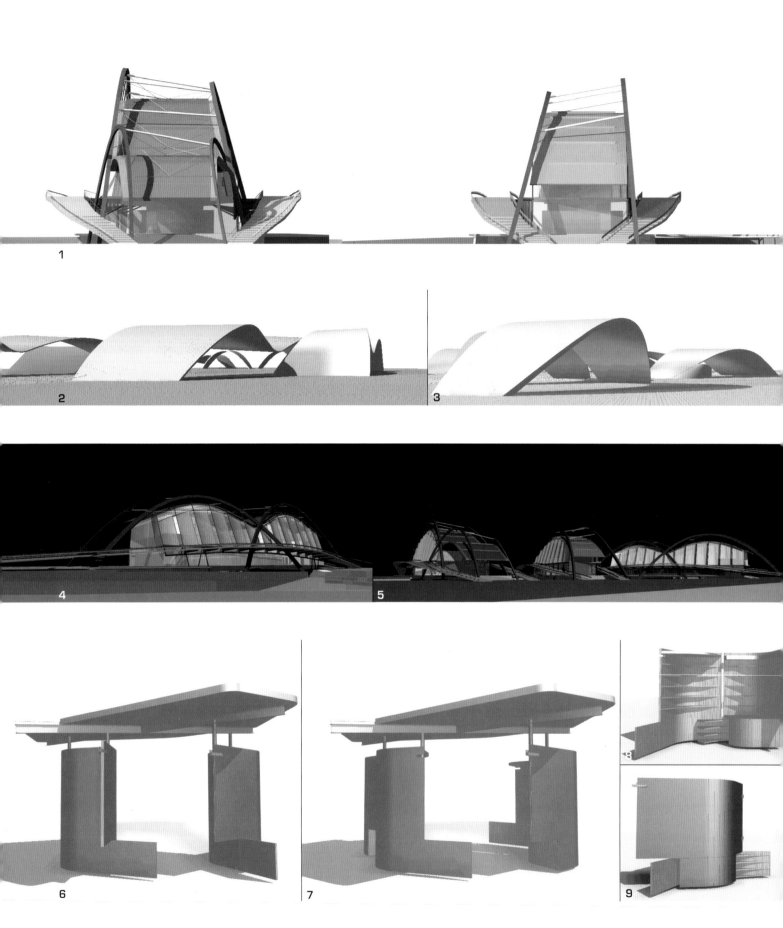

Fairgrounds, Jorge Vergara Cultural and Business Center, Guadalajara, Mexico: 1 Both buildings and bridges, these structures connect the Fairgrounds section with a central square; 2&3 Undulating concrete strips act as roofs for different concession stands; 4&5 The exteriors of these buildings are metal; the interiors, wood; 6–9 Fairground stands.

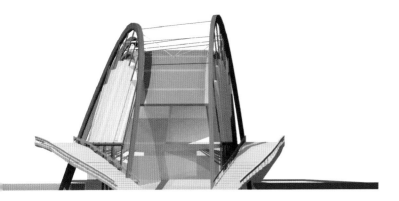

Pedestrian Bridge, Petrer, Alicante, Spain: 1–3 The bridge is made up of three intersecting steel arches which intersect and support a platform halfway along the route. All elements are interconnected. Lights intermingle with the wooden lathes of the roof; the undulating, origami-like stretches of wood and steel are sometimes places to walk, sometimes places to sit. Always, the orientation of the seated pedestrian is toward the mountains.

Ses Estaciones Parc, Palma de Mallorca, Mallorca, Spain: There are no straight lines; everything was resolved with curves.
1&2 Metal arcs serve as giant planters for flowers; 3 The pedestrian perspective on concrete fountains, placed at different levels, changes as one walks along.

Regina Pizzinini
United States of America

"I believe in architecture as an object of beauty, composed of the spirit of a certain place and the imagination of one or more individuals. This object of beauty should evoke joy, positive feelings, questions, and surprises—the use of it should become a new experience."

PROFESSIONAL HISTORY

Regina Pizzinini graduated from the University of Innsbruck in 1983 with a degree in architecture and interior design. Her practical training during those undergraduate years was with Professor of Architecture Josef Lackner. In 1985 she received a master's in architecture from UCLA's School of Architecture and Urban Planning. While at UCLA, Pizzinini served as a teaching assistant with Charles Jencks in 1984 and a research assistant with Charles Moore in 1985. She also received practical training between 1983 and 1986 with Moore, Ruble Yudell Architects and Planners.

From 1985 to 1987 Pizzinini served as assistant professor of architecture and interior design at the Academy of Applied Arts in Vienna. In 1988, she lectured on building design with Landscape Studio, UCLA. Pizzinini has also lectured with UCLA's Building Design Exchange Studio and the University Iberoamericano in Mexico City since 1989.

In 1989, Pizzinini and Leon Luxemburg established offices in Santa Monica and Luxembourg; in 1995 they opened a third office in Vienna.

Selected Publications

Architects of the New Millennium. Mulgrave, Australia: The Images Publishing Group, 2000.

Rew, Terry. *Feng Shui Today.* New York: Watson-Guptill Publications, 2000.

Pizzinini, Regina and Leon Luxemburg. *House Design (Volume, Geometry, Color).* Mulgrave, Australia: The Images Publishing Group, 1998.

"Short-Order Remodel." *Los Angeles Times Magazine*, Home section, 5 October 1997.

"'Villa Petite': Award Winning Architecture." *International Architecture Yearbook.* Mulgrave, Australia: The Images Publishing Group, 1997.

Cooper, Guy and Gordon Taylor. *Paradise Transformed: The Private Garden for the Twenty-First Century.* New York: The Monacelli Press, 1996.

FIRM PROFILE

International architectural practices are common, but the ten-year partnership of Regina Pizzinini and Leon Luxemburg differs from most in the regularity with which they shuttle back and forth between their offices in California and Europe. In their mobility, as in the joyous exuberance of their residential projects, they are true heirs of the late Charles Moore, who in 1983 inspired them to move from Austria to Los Angeles, and who invited them to study and work with him.

Like most young architects, Pizzinini and Luxemburg started small, with a guest house and remodeling projects, gradually moving to residences and competing for the design of public buildings. Pizzinini, Luxemburg, and Tryggvi Thorsteinsson, who became a partner in the Los Angeles office in 1998, have designed residences of growing scale and complexity, playing on variations of recurring themes: simple geometric forms, interlocking volumes, and primary colors. The versatility of these architects is shown by the extraordinary variety of buildings they have designed—residences, both large and small; housing, public and private; West Coast health centers; a museum of flight; urban redevelopment; a photo studio; even a monastery—and the range of project types they are interested in— from urban planning and environmental studies to large-scale institutional and governmental complexes.

Selected Clients

California Health and Rejuvenation Centers, *California*

City of Vienna, *Austria*

Don Wallace Radio Museum, *Rancho Palos Verdes, California*

Monastery Marienthal, ecological center, *Luxembourg*

Western Museum of Flight, *Los Angeles*

DESIGN STATEMENT

House Niederthai, Niederthai, Austria, 1991–1993

Every project is a fresh challenge to develop and express my design philosophy. Every new task is, in a sense, an experiment, based on a new exploration of the exciting spaces and unusual experiences I have created with past projects. To take these experiences one step further—to explore new scales and compositions during the design process—requires hard work and involves frustration, surprise, joy, and satisfaction, leading, ultimately, to a successful project and happy clients.

The most challenging task for me as an architect was to be my own client. The program for House Niederthai was uncertain, the design possibilities endless, and the goals very high. There were outside pressures—from my family and from the professional world—as well as internal pressures created by my own ambitious goals for what I perceived as the ultimate experiment. The budget restrictions were, of course, also there. I was able finally to put them aside, only to find out in the end that I will be paying off the final expenses for the rest of my life.

The site for House Niederthai was also the most challenging that I've faced: a property in my home village, in the mountainous state of Tirol, in western Austria. Growing up in this remote village, where a small community of farmhouses provided a backdrop for a few tourists, my relationship with the serene setting was not always friendly. When I left the village to study I was ready for city life, people, and action. I returned many years later, after traveling all over the world, and had to re-evaluate the existing qualities of the landscape, which I now saw with different eyes and a new appreciation. I was looking for serenity, quiet, and nature.

I had worked for many years in Los Angeles and Vienna, where I had developed my own architectural expression. The spaces I wanted to create had little in common with the needs of the traditional farmhouses. I wanted to find an aesthetic that would allow for exciting spaces on the inside, interact with the landscape, and allow the whole building to be composed within the context of the natural surroundings. My task was to rediscover, use, and become enriched by traditional values, and at the same time to transform the architectural vernacular to fit my own philosophies— to take my architectural goals this one step further. House Niederthai involved the same issues as all my other projects: hard work, frustration, the unexpected, satisfaction, and ultimate success. This time, however, I am the happy client, able to enjoy the spaces and surprises repeatedly, always discovering something new.

ILLUSTRATED PROJECTS

Kieffer Photo Studio, City of Luxembourg, Luxembourg, 1994–1996

Villa Petite, Bridel, Luxembourg, 1991–1993

Corman Guest House, Santa Monica, California, 1989–1992

House Niederthai, Niederthai, Austria, 1994–1996

[Below] **Kieffer Photo Studio, City of Luxembourg, Luxembourg:** View of the exterior, with tapered yellow tower marking the entrance and red frame marking upstairs office. Every angle of the building, along with the sculpture in the forecourt, draws attention and offers a gift to the street. Photo credit: Jean-Paul Kieffer

[Above] **Villa Petite, Bridel, Luxembourg:** 1 Interior view of main floor and yellow bridge above. From the bridge, an angled screen wall leads to a red, windowed sleeping bay that faces north so the view is always backlit. Huge windows make the interior feel expansive, borrowing space from the garden; 2 Exterior view, showing double sweep of yellow stairs, projecting red bay, and jauntily tiled circular roof with fanned logs that relate to the surrounding trees. Photo credit: Gert von Bassewitz

[Below] **Corman Guest House, Santa Monica, California:** 1 Side view of library and red walls emerging from the lawn. A whimsical metal canopy juts from the studio; within, a cradle of beams filters the skylight; 2 Intensely colorful red walls and narrow yellow stairs provide a dramatic entrance, later offset by the cooler colors and natural materials of the interior. Photo credit: Dominique Vorillon

[Above] **House Niederthai, Niederthai, Austria:** 1 Interior view, showing vertiginous stairs leading from main living space to galleries, suspended yellow cube bedroom, and models. The stairs invite you to climb and make discoveries, as if scrambling up a rock face; 2 Interior of suspended red bay with postcard view; 3 Exterior front view, showing bowed metal roof; white walls; expansive, unshaded windows; and suspended red bay. A double flight of yellow stairs leads to the living room terrace and symbolizes the earth excavated during construction. Photo credit: Gert von Bassewitz

Kazuyo Sejima

Japan

"I want to make architecture that matches the rhythms of our daily lives, although it is by no means easy to keep up with the speed of the age."

PROFESSIONAL HISTORY

Kazuyo Sejima graduated from Japan's Women's University, Tokyo, in 1981, with a master's degree in architecture. In 1982, she joined Toyo Ito Architects & Associates, where she stayed until establishing her own practice, Kazuyo Sejima & Associates, in 1987. Within a year, the firm received the first of numerous awards, the *Space Design* review's Kajima Award, for PLATFORMS I and II. PLATFORM I was also awarded the Yoshioka Prize and a special prize for residential architecture by the Tokyo Architect Association, both in 1989. In 1992, Sejima was named Young Architect of the Year by the Architectural Institute of Japan (AIJ). Other award-winning designs during the early 1990s were a women's dormitory at the University of Hawaii (Kenneth F. Brown Asia Pacific Culture and Architecture Design Award, 1995) and a forest villa (AIJ's Architecture of the Year, 1994). In 1994, twelve of her projects were exhibited at Gallery Ma in Tokyo. Sejima has been a visiting lecturer at the Japan Women's University, Kyoto University, and the Tokyo Institute of Technology.

In 1995 Sejima co-founded the design collaboration SANAA (Kazuyo Sejima + Ryue Nishizawa & Associates) with Ryue Nishizawa, who studied architecture at Yokohama National University, receiving his master's in architecture in 1990. SANAA's award-winning designs include the Hirosaka Geijyutsu Gai design proposal for the Museum of Contemporary Art in Kanazawa, Japan, and the Stadstheater Almere in the Netherlands, both in 1999; Edifici-mondo, designed in a competition for the restoration of the old town section of Salerno, Italy, in 1998; and Multimedia Studio in Gifu Prefecture, Japan, which was awarded the AIJ Prize in 1998.

Selected Publications

"Kazuyo Sejima, Ryue Nishizawa 1995–2000." *El Croquis*, no. 99, 2000.

"Gifu Kitagawa Apartment." *The Japan Architect*, Spring 1999.

"Kazuyo Sejima + Ryue Nishizawa." *The Japan Architect*, no. 35, 1999.

GA Sejima Kazuyo Dokuhon. Tokyo: A.D.A. Edita, 1998.

"Forms of Indeterminacy." *Casabella*, July/August 1998.

"Mountain Minimalism." *Architectural Review*, May 1998.

"Kazuyo Sejima 1988–1996." *El Croquis*, no. 77, 1996.

FIRM PROFILE

The title of the 1998 *Casabella* article about the work of Kazuyo Sejima, "Forms of Indeterminacy," provides important insight into the work of both Kazuyo Sejima & Associates and SANAA: In their designs the materials, the orientation, the light sources, the shapes and spatial relation—all the architectural elements—create a sense of fluidity in which the relationships between viewer and structure, between building and surroundings, between interior and exterior, seem not to be fixed, but to change depending on where one is and where one is going, what time of day it is, and what the weather and light are like.

Sejima and Nishizawa are both committed to architecture that is informed by local context—both environmental and social, including all the ambiguities created by changing conditions in our natural and urban environments—but that avoids a reliance on details that, as Sejima puts it, are "the products of pre-existing relations." For example, in one of their prototype designs for a housing project, the gardens are placed at different elevations and at different positions throughout the facade, representing a new approach to the traditional Japanese garden while maintaining the importance of the gardens to the overall design.

In addition to numerous innovative private residences, Kazuyo Sejima & Associates has designed large apartment complexes; public structures, such as theaters, museums, and restoration projects; educational buildings, such as the multimedia workshop and a dormitory; and even a police box.

ILLUSTRATED PROJECTS

Gifu Kitagata Apartments, 1st Stage, Motosu, Gifu Prefecture, Japan, 1998 (Kazuyo Sejima & Associates): Part of a large-scale public housing reconstruction project and collaboration of four female architects, under the coordination of the Arata Isozaki Atelier. The buildings were designed as thin slabs following the perimeter of the site, with complex and varied elevations that were intended to avoid the monotonous, monolithic volumes of most high-rise housing.

Villa in the Forest, Nagano Prefecture, Japan, 1994 (Kazuyo Sejima & Associates): Located two hours outside Tokyo by car, this forest home of a gallery owner was also to serve as an atelier. The plan was designed with two circles, one inside the other—the center circle forming the gallery and the surrounding ring the main living space. The two spaces have different characters but are connected by architectural fittings.

Park Café, Ibaraki Prefecture, Japan, 1998 (Kazuyo Sejima & Ryue Nisizhawa/SANAA): A café for visitors of the surrounding park, this structure was intended as a "place" within the natural landscape, rather than an "object" (building) set within it. Sliding glass doors allow interior spaces to become semi-exterior in warm weather. Four internal walls and all tabletops were finished with mirrorlike materials to fill the interior with reflections of the surrounding greenery and blue sky.

Multimedia Studio, Gifu Prefecture, Japan, 1997 (Kazuyo Sejima & Ryue Nishizawa/SANAA): This building is located on the campus of a prefectural school for media arts. The functions of this building include ateliers, a studio, and a gallery, where artists involved in computer art and multimedia art can stay for specified periods. The roof-garden linked to the campus serves as the entrance.

Gifu Kitagata Apartments, 1st Stage, Motosu, Gifu Prefecture, Japan: 1 Each apartment's varied composition is invisible when walking along the shared corridor, making it impossible to know which door is for which unit; 2 North façade. Terraces cut through the entire building, offering glimpses of the opposite side and reducing the visual impression of massiveness; 3 Ground floor plan, showing the building as a thin slab running around the site's perimeter; 4 View of the dining room. Each unit has a terrace, eat-in kitchen, and bedrooms, all lined up along the side receiving the most natural light and linked by a narrow sunroom on the front; 5 View of a terrace. Photo credit: Nobuaki Nakagawa

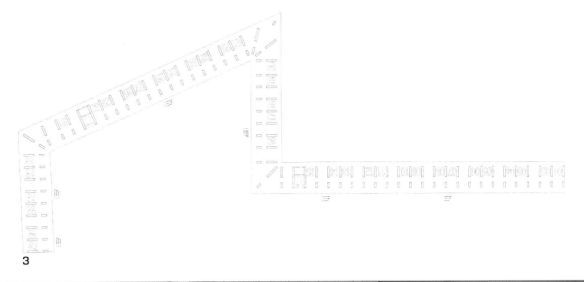

3

4

5

[Right] **Park Café/SANAA, Ibaraki Prefecture, Japan:** View of north elevation, showing the thin roof of Keystone-steel plate supported by steel pipe columns and the sliding glass doors. Photo credit: Nobuaki Nakagawa

Villa in the Forest, Nagano Prefecture, Japan: 1 East view; 2 View of the atelier in the center, with abundant natural light coming from above; 3 View of the outer circle, containing the kitchen, dining area, and bedrooms. Openings in the outer wall, with its endless circulation, provide different views of the surrounding forest. Photo credit: Motoi Niki

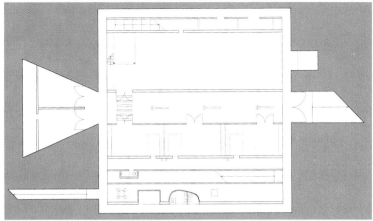

[Above] **Multimedia Workshop/SANAA, Gifu Prefecture, Japan:**
Basement plan.

Laurinda Spear
United States of America

Photo credit: David Peterson Studios, courtesy HBF Textiles

"Fundamentally, I am always interested in the artistic aspect of any project. People should feel an emotion when they see one of our buildings. I want to touch a person's heart. Whether a design taps into local culture or the spirit of the times, there has to be something that elicits an emotional response for me to feel that I've done my job well."

PROFESSIONAL HISTORY

Laurinda Spear has practiced architecture with Bernardo Fort-Brescia, her husband, since the two founded Arquitectonica (ARQ) in Miami in 1977. Since then, ARQ has been responsible for scores of competition-winning designs, including the US Embassy in Lima, Peru; the Philips Arena in Atlanta; the American Airlines Arena in Miami, Disney All-Star Resorts; and Westin's 45-story hotel on 42nd Street's E Walk in New York City (scheduled for completion in 2002).

Spear has also worked on designs at a smaller scale, such as a line of eye-catching laminates for Formica with names like Millennium, Cosmos, and Rain Forest; hardware for Valli & Valli; and watches and clocks, including her famous mirror timepieces. Most recently she has designed lines of vinyl wall covering for Wolf Gordon, architectural glass for Skyline, and a ceiling fan for the Modern Fan Company.

Spear received her bachelor of arts in fine arts from Brown University in 1972 and a master of arts in architecture from Columbia University in 1975. She received the Rome Prize in Architecture in 1978 and was made a fellow of the American Institute of Architects (AIA) in 1992. She has lectured widely, and her work has been exhibited around the world.

Selected Awards

Award for Excellence, Built Category: Miami AIA, Festival Walk Hong Kong, 1999; Florida AIA, Dijon Performing Arts Center, 1999

Interior Design Magazine Hall of Fame, 1999

Award of Excellence, Unbuilt Category, Florida AIA, American Airlines Arena, 1998

Firm of the Year Award, Florida AIA, 1998

Silver Medal for Design Excellence, Miami AIA, 1998

Selected Publications

Vonier, F. and T. Vonier. "Auditorium de Dijon." *Architectural Record*, May 1999.

Stein, Karen D. "A Fortress with No Apologies." *Architectural Record*, October 1996: 78–87.

Gandee, Charles. "Plunging Ahead." *Vogue*, August 1995: 226–231, 271.

Muschamp, Herbert. "A Flare for Fantasy: *Miami Vice* Meets 42nd Street." *The New York Times*, 21 May 1995: Section 2, p. 1.

FIRM PROFILE

Arquitectonica (ARQ) is based in Miami and New York, with offices in Los Angeles, Paris, Hong Kong, Shanghai, Manila, Lima, Buenos Aires, and São Paulo. Since its founding in 1977, ARQ has developed an international practice recognized for excellence and innovation. The firm is best known for its creative ability to design projects with memorable imagery and regional identity.

ARQ had a fast start. Its first built project, the Pink House (1978), immediately caught the attention of architectural and popular audiences worldwide, and proved that the firm was capable of designing and building large projects with radical new ideas. The building's skycourt, with a palm tree, red corkscrew stairs, and blue pool, became a symbol of Miami's own new architecture and a rallying flag for a new generation of modernists fighting for survival in a postmodernist/revivalist era.

The Banque de Luxembourg Headquarters (1994) was the firm's first project completed in Europe, and represented ARQ's response to a highly defined urban context. The building is an abstract collage: a limestone rectangular volume with punched windows aligns with the street edge and cornice lines, a conical glass tower completes the axis of the boulevard, and a black granite trunk holds the various elements together.

ARQ has created its own brand of rigorous modernism and populist expressionism. The work is invariably based on ideas, and the resultant concepts are expressed with graphic clarity and formal legibility. The firm has a reputation of maintaining the direct involvement of its principals in the design of all projects, and is committed to the design of buildings that meet functional requirements while incorporating state-of-the-art technology.

Selected Clients

Banking: Banque de Luxembourg, Banco de Credito del Peru.

Development: Catellus, Helmsley-Spear, Tishman Urban Development, Tishman-Speyer

Hotels: Four Seasons, Hilton International, Marriott, Ritz Carlton, St. Regis, The Walt Disney Company, Westin

New Media: iXL, Pacific Century Cyberworks

Retail: The Mills Corporation, Swire Properties

Sports and Entertainment: Miami Basketball Properties, MTV Latino, NBC, Sony, Turner Sports and Entertainment

United States Government: Department of State and General Services Administration

DESIGN STATEMENT

Dijon Performing Arts Center, Dijon, France

In 1991, ARQ won an international competition to design both the master plan and all of the specified buildings for a modern exhibition and business center at the edge of the medieval city of Dijon. The centerpiece was the Performing Arts Center, completed in 1998. We designed the building as a sweeping curve that bridges across the Boulevard de Champagne, the avenue that exits Dijon toward the famous countryside of Bourgnone. The building functions as a gateway to the city, reinstating in a modern abstraction the city walls. The modern expression is reinforced by the sense of movement of the building, and the fact that it is suspended off the ground. This architectural "swoosh" form slides over a lower piece that hugs the edges of a small triangular block, which is separated from the rest of the complex. The upper volume also acts as a bridge leading to the urban citadel, the "Cité des Affaires," or "City of Business."

France has codes that dictate the amount of natural light required for all habitable spaces, so we designed an elliptical void, open to the sky, marking the center of the lobby and allowing light to pass inside the building and through it to the street below. There is also an emphasis on longevity and the use of permanent materials, so we chose to clad the exterior in Chassagne, a local limestone, while using grey and red granites throughout the interior. The geometry of the interior patterns is derived from the curved plan of the building and can be found on the terrazzo floors, the wood inlay of the walls, and the balcony railings. The opera/symphony hall's interior walls, clad in various types and shades of folding wood planes, form a series of terracing plateaus. Suspended over them are gold-rubbed acoustical pillows separated by crevices filled with cool light crystals that serve as modern-day chandeliers. Warm light glowing from below the seats makes the audience part of the decor. The acoustics are adjustable and have a reverberation time of two seconds.

ILLUSTRATED PROJECTS

Dijon Performing Arts Center, Dijon, France, 1991–1998

Festival Walk, Hong Kong, 1993–1998

Dijon Performing Arts Center, Dijon, France: 1 Detail; 2 Southwest facade with elevated reception terrace, metal sculpture, and street level garden promenade; 3 Grand Hall Auditorium, view from stage; 4 West facade, twilight view of Performing Arts Center bridging across Boulevard de Champagne, John Bouhey Place; 5 Elevated entrance hall with dominating panoramic views of city; 6 Lower west foyer and café; 7 Performing Arts Center, entrance level (elevated). Photo credits: Paul Maurer (1–6); courtesy of Arquitectonica (7)

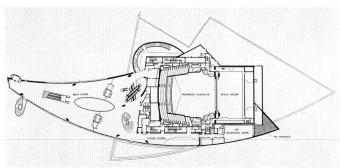

7

Festival Walk, Hong Kong: 1 Exterior; 2 Concept design for east elevation; 3 Concept design for west elevation; 4 The Canyon, top level, view to east; 5 Exterior, detail of glazing at north corner; 6 The Glacier, ice rink at bottom with food court on elliptical bridges suspended overhead; 7 The Glacier, ice rink with view to east, with diagonal across ceiling marking offices above; 8 The River atrium. Photo credits: courtesy Arquitectonica (1, 2, 3–5); Ralph Thomas (4,6–8)

Billie Tsien
United States of America

"I believe architecture is the coming together of art and life, formed by a combination of hope, discipline, and love. What we are trying to do is make shelter—shelter for the body, and shelter for the soul."

PROFESSIONAL HISTORY

Billie Tsien received her undergraduate degree in fine arts from Yale in 1971, and her master's in architecture from UCLA in 1977. Between 1971 and 1975, she was a painter and taught art at a private girl's school. Since 1979, she has taught at the Southern California Institute of Architecture, Parsons School of Design in New York City, Yale, Harvard's Gradate School of Design, and the University of Texas. In 1977, Tsien started working with Tod Willliams, now her husband, and in 1986 they co-founded Tod Williams Billie Tsien and Associates.

As with all young practices in New York City, the primary focus for many years was interior work, providing an opportunity to think about details in a very concentrated way. This kind of training—a long, slow evolution in scale—is the foundation of how the office works today. All parts must speak together as a whole, in one voice. The studio works together in one room. This collaborative "family" effort requires a unity and sense of commitment to the work and to each other. The one voice is in fact made of many voices.

Tsien has a particular interest in work that bridges art and architecture. She is on the board of the Public Art Fund, the Architectural League of New York, and New York's Municipal Art Society. In 1998, Tsien and Tod Williams shared the Jane and Bruce Graham Chair at the University of Pennsylvania.

Selected Awards

Chrysler Award for Innovation in Design, 1998

American Institute of Architects (AIA) National Honor Award, for the Neurosciences Institute, 1997

AIA New York Chapter Medal of Honor Award, 1996

Arnold W. Brunner Memorial Prize, American Academy of Arts & Letters, 1996

Time Magazine Best of Design Award, for the Neurosciences Institute, 1996

Federal Design Achievement Award, Presidential Design Awards, National Endowment for the Arts, for the St. Louis Light Rail, 1995

Environments Design Distinction Award, *International Design Magazine* Annual Design Review, for Quiet Light: Akari Light Sculptures at Takashimaya, 1995

Selected Publications

Futagawa, Yoshio. "Tod Williams, Billie Tsien." *GA Houses*, January 2000: 10–17.

Williams, Tod and Billie Tsien. *WorkLife*. New York: The Monacelli Press, 2000.

Martin Finio, ed. *Williams Tsien Works. 2G Monograph No.9*. Barcelona: Editorial Gistavo Gili, sa., 1998.

Ryan, Raymund. "Nature: fabric: beauty." *Architecture and Urbanism*, June 1997: 54–59.

Zevon, Susan. "A Cleansing Experience." *House Beautiful*, September 1996: 134–135.

FIRM PROFILE

The work of Tod Williams Billie Tsien and Associates bridges different worlds—across theory and practice, across architecture and the fine arts. Together, they have produced works with artists such as Jackie Ferrara, Mary Miss, and Elyn Zimmerman. In 1990, the firm designed a movable set and costumes for a commissioned dance project at the Hetmuziek Theater in Amsterdam, which had its American premiere at New York's City Center in 1991. They've also designed sets and costumes for the Elisa Monte Dance Company in New York.

In 1989 and 1990, Williams and Tsien produced the provocative traveling exhibition *Domestic Arrangements: A Lab Report*, sponsored by the Walker Art Center in Minneapolis. The installation explored how issues of social idealism and aesthetic discipline formed the early Modern movement, opening at the Walker Art Museum and then traveling to the Whitney Museum of American Art, the Cleveland Center for Contemporary Art, and the Power Plant in Toronto. The firm has also designed traveling shows for the Noguchi Foundation, created a master plan for the Noguchi Museum on Long Island, and designed the permanent installation of the Museum of the Chinese in the Americas in New York.

In summer 1994, Williams and Tsien presented *Quiet Light*, a traveling installation of their own luminous fiberglass screens and Isamu Noguchi's Akari light sculptures. Other completed projects include several residences; the Hereford College facilities at the University of Virginia; a major addition to the Phoenix Art Museum; and a science building and aquatic center for the Emma Willard School in Troy, New York. The firm's most widely published projects include the downtown branch of the Whitney Museum of American Art and Spiegel Pool House in New York City, Feinberg Hall at Princeton University,

and its award-winning Neurosciences Institute in La Jolla, California.

The firm's work borders on minimalism and pays careful attention to context, detail, and the subtleties of a subdued but rich materiality. Current projects include aquatic centers for the Cranbrook School in Bloomfield Hills, Michigan; the East Asian Studies building at the University of California, Berkeley; the new Museum of American Folk Art in New York City; and the Student Art Center at Johns Hopkins University in Baltimore.

Selected Clients

Cranbrook Educational Community, *Bloomfield Hills, Michigan*

Emma Willard School, *Troy, New York*

Johns Hopkins University, *Baltimore, Maryland*

The Museum of American Folk Art, *New York City*

Neurosciences Institute, the Scripps Research Institute, *La Jolla, California*

Phoenix Art Museum and Museum Theater, *Phoenix, Arizona*

DESIGN STATEMENT

The most challenging aspect of any project has to do with the balance between art and use.

In each project, it is the same and it is different. How do you infuse pragmatism with dreams?

ILLUSTRATED PROJECTS

Rifkind House, New York City, 1998: This house is comprised of four volumes—the public spaces, a master bedroom wing, a guest wing, and a planting and storage shed—that unfold as one walks through or around it. Its relationship to the landscape results in changing qualities of light and shadow throughout the day and seasons.

Museum of American Folk Art, New York City, slated for completion in 2001: The museum's new home will be faced with cast panels of *tombasil*, a white bronze. Light has been an important consideration: The front was designed to quietly reflect a golden light as the sun passes from east to west and "cut-throughs" will filter natural light into interior spaces.

Quiet Light: Akari Light Sculptures at Takashimaya, traveling installation, 1994: In this "garden" for the Akari lamps of Isamu Noguchi, fiberglass screens define spaces and create a path through the exhibit. The lamps glow through the screens, revealing their shapes while concealing details until visitors pass by.

Rifkind House, New York City: 1 Section plan; 2 Master bathroom bench and shower wall; 3 Exterior of living room with New York bluestone fireplace, small reading loft above, and glass passageway; 4 Site plan, showing the four distinct volumes; 5 West elevation of entry with mature pitch pines in foreground. Photo credit: Michael Moran

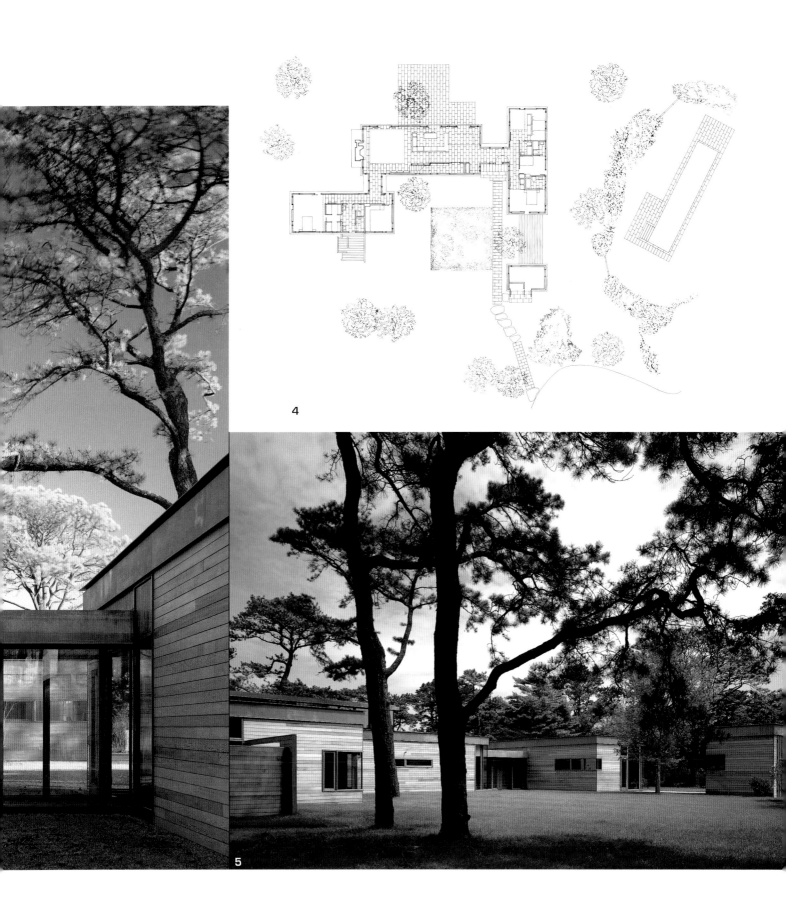

4

5

Museum of American Folk Art, New York City: 1 Ground floor plan; 2 Photo collage of the museum's location, with MoMA next door; 3 Model of the facade; 4 Cutaway section model, showing the skylight that caps the building. Photo credit: courtesy Tod Williams Billie Tsien and Associates [2]; Michael Moran [3&4]

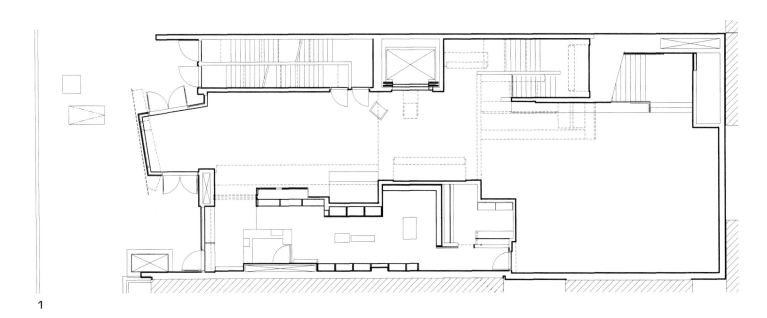

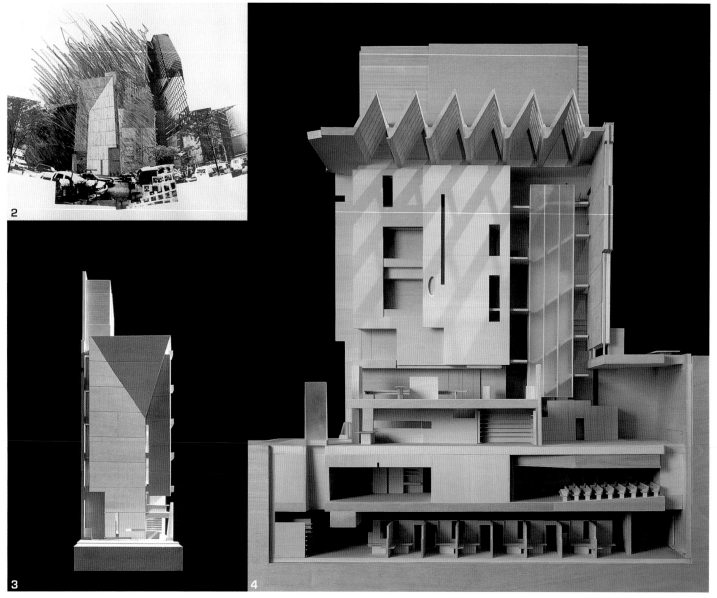

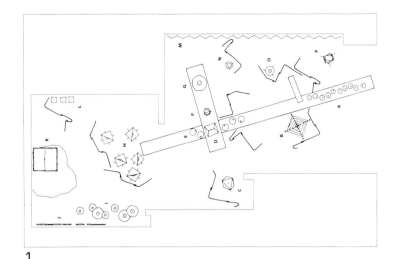

**Quiet Light: Akari Light Sculptures at Takashimaya
(traveling installation):** 1 Floor plan of installation;
2 The Akari "garden," with translucent fiberglass screens.
Photo credit: Michael Moran

Nanako Umemoto
United States of America

"In our work we have attempted to go beyond conventional notions of program, form, and organization. This is not an idiosyncratic wish, but one enabled by emerging models of thought and technique."

PROFESSIONAL HISTORY

Nanako Umemoto studied urban and landscape design at the Osaka University of Art in Japan, receiving her bachelor of arts in 1975. After graduating, she was appointed an assistant professor at the university, teaching between 1975 and 1976. She also practiced with various Japanese firms, namely Masanori Akira Architects in Osaka and Sadao Nagaoka Design, Inc. in Tokyo.

In 1979, Umemoto came to the United States to study architecture at New York City's Cooper Union, receiving a bachelor's degree in architecture in 1983. Between 1983 and 1984, she practiced with Debora Reiser Design, Inc., in New York, and Minoru Yamasaki Architects in Michigan. The following year, she worked as a visiting artist at the American Academy in Rome, Italy. In 1986, Umemoto and her husband, Jesse Reiser, founded Reiser + Umemoto in New York City.

Umemoto has also held various academic posts. Between 1989 and 1996 she served as a guest critic at Columbia University, Tulane University, and Illinois Institute of Technology. In 1995, she was appointed an adjunct assistant professor of architecture at Columbia University's Advanced Studio, where she taught until 1999. She also headed a workshop at the Universidad Torcuato di Tella in Buenos Aires, Argentina in 1998, and has lectured extensively around the world.

Selected Awards

Academy Award in Architecture, American Academy of Arts and Letters, 2000

Graham Foundation Grant, 2000

Daimler/Chrysler Award for Excellence in Design, 1999

Finalist in the International Foundation for the Canadian Centre for Architecture (IFCCA) Competition, 1999

New York State Council of the Arts Grant in Architecture, the Architectural League of New York, 1999

Progressive Architecture Award, 1998

Selected Publications

Kong, Chul. "The Works of Reiser and Umemoto." *Space*, January 1999.

Rappapport, Nina. "The Reiser + Umemoto Plan for the East River." *Oculus*, May/June 1999.

Reiser, Jesse and Nanako Umemoto. "East River Corridor Project." *Architecture and Urbanism*, May 1999.

Reiser, Jesse and Nanako Umemoto. "Music Theater, Graz." *Architectural Design*, March/April 1999.

Reiser, Jesse and Nanako Umemoto. "Riding on the Edge: On the Design Study for Manhattan's Franklin D. Roosevelt Drive." *Daidalos*, Summer 1999.

Benjamin, Andrew, with introduction by Daniel Libeskind. *Reiser + Umemoto: Recent Projects*. London: John Wiley & Son Ltd., 1998.

FIRM PROFILE

Nanako Umemoto and Jesse Reiser have been practicing in New York as Reiser + Umemoto since 1986. Reiser + Umemoto deals with projects of many different scales and sites, from domestic to urban, from furniture to landscape, pushing the limits of form, organization, and function at each of these scales.

In 1990, the firm's study of the New York State water supply and Croton Aqueduct corridor, funded by the National Endowment for the Arts, established it as a specialist in large-scale, infrastructural urban developments. In 1998 the firm developed a proposal for the riverfront of Manhattan's East River, and in 1999 it was selected as one of five participants in an IFCCA competition focusing on Manhattan's West Side.

Reiser + Umemoto approaches each project as part of an ongoing study of relationships between architecture, territory, and systems of distribution. By working on projects of varying scales, the firm seeks to open structures that were formerly rigid and inflexible, and to integrate domains that have historically been understood as distinct from one another.

Selected Clients

Graz Music Theater, *Graz, Austria*

I. Wolf (landscape and garden structures), *Sandy Point, New York*

Sklar Residential Loft, *New York City*

Spence Centers for Women's Health, *Chevy Chase, Maryland and Wellesley, Massachusetts*

DESIGN STATEMENT

Each project is exceptionally challenging as we push the limits of form, organization, and function at various scales.

When designing the Spence Centers for Women's Health in Chevy Chase, Maryland and Wellesley, Massachusetts in 1995, Reiser + Umemoto used a combination of sculptural forms and flowing circulation in a relatively small envelope, so as to contain a wide variety of functions. Curved walls were made of ruled surfaces constructed of sheetrock on metal studs, making the sculptural forms simple and economical to build. With ruled surfaces, each stud remains straight as the entire assembly twists and turns, making this kind of geometry entirely consistent with the methods of sheetrock construction. In fact, as the firm continued to pursue this technique in other health centers, it found that as builders became comfortable with the idea it became less and less expensive to produce forms of ever-greater complexity. In this design, the challenge was to create complex forms with simplicity of means, creating a strong yet graduated distinction between public and private areas. The visitor moves fluidly between the active public reception area, the semi-public areas (for exercises, classes, and so on), and the very private consultation and examination area behind.

For a design on the urban scale—a proposal for Manhattan's West Side convergence—the firm again used flow and movement to organize form and function for various scales. The design started with a very simple flow diagram that moved from east to west across the massive site, then applied the same diagram to ideas surrounding structure, material, program, and organization. This simple method of diagramming a site's abstract flow becomes extremely complex and interesting when it interacts with the realities and existing conditions of the site. The resulting proposal yielded an intensely varied and unique public space, with diverse programmatic and formal conditions.

ILLUSTRATED PROJECTS

East River Corridor, New York City, 1998: Manhattan's East River waterfront is defined in three zones: urban (i.e. the FDR Drive, a high-speed vehicular artery); local, in which residents establish intimate, long-term uses of the waterfront; and the intermediate scale of public amenities.

Proposal for West Side Convergence, New York City, 1999: An international jury selected five finalists, including Reiser + Umemoto, to make proposals for one of the last undeveloped areas of midtown Manhattan.

East River Corridor, New York City: 1 View of proposed Spaceframe Sports Complex south of East River Park and just east of the FDR Drive; 2&3 View of new Butterfly Pier Ferry Terminal south of the South Street Seaport, an example of the local scale; 4 Site/project events plan; 5 View of new entertainment complex for East Harlem. Photo credit: Reiser + Umemoto, RUR Architecture P.C.

BATTERY PARK CITY

BATTERY MARITIME
BUILDING

FDR DRIVE BELOW GRADE

pedestrian esplanade
ascending from Battery
Maritime building to new
Ferry Terminal

local car/bike loop
starting point

pedestrian path

FDR DRIVE ELEVATED

BUTTERFLY PIER
-ferry terminal
-public/private marina
-indoor/outdoor market area
-water taxi stand
-commercial spaces
vehicular access
to ferry terminal

local car/bike loop

pedestrian path

esplanade descending
to South Street Seaport

SOUTH STREET SEAPORT/
FULTON FISH MARKET

BOARDWALKS
-open programming
-market area

BROOKYLN BRIDGE

BOARDWALKS
-open programming
-market area
-water taxi stand

4

5

West Side Convergence, New York City: 1 View of proposed project from above the James Farley Post Office; 2 View over rooftop of proposed Spaceframe structure; 3 View of relationship of project to Jacob Javitz Center at 34th Street; 4 Aerial view of project from the south; 5 Close-up view of proposed Spaceframe structure, which will enclose cultural programs. Photo credit: Reiser + Umemoto, RUR Architecture P.C.

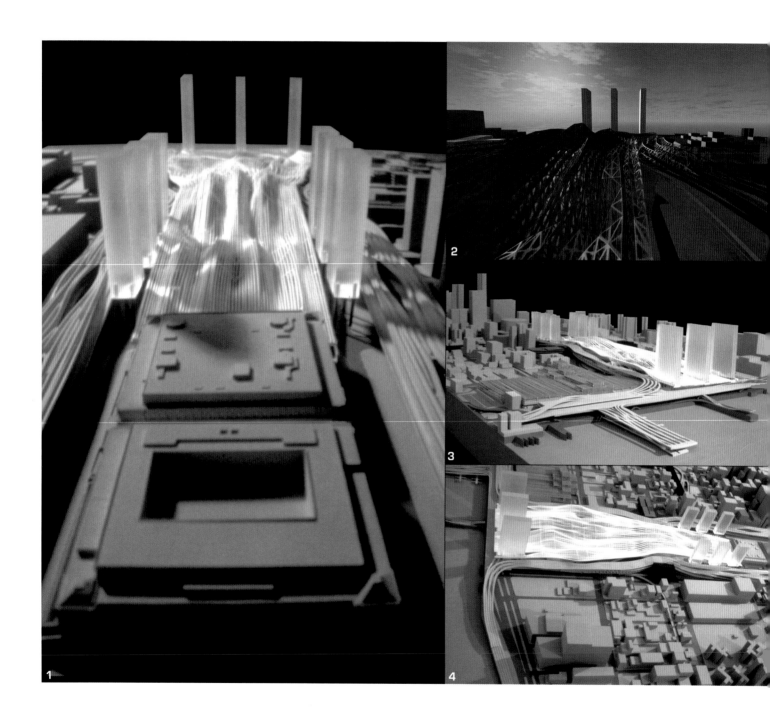

Sarah Wigglesworth
United Kingdom

"I believe that the increased participation of women in the making of the environment—as users, clients, and professionals—can change the culture of architecture and forge new ways to think about how we want the places around us to be."

PROFESSIONAL HISTORY

Sarah Wigglesworth studied architecture at Cambridge University, graduating with distinction in 1983. In 1991, after a number of years practicing in London, she and colleague Jeremy Till were awarded a joint Fulbright Arts Fellowship in Architecture for a year's research in the United States.

In 1993, Wigglesworth founded her own practice, Sarah Wigglesworth Architects, in London. Since then, her professional profile has continued to rise, partly as a result of the Straw House project, to be completed at the end of 2000 (see pages 172–173). In 1998, she edited issue no. 134 of *Architectural Design* and orchestrated a symposium of the same name at the Institute of Contemporary Arts in London. Also in 1998, Wigglesworth was chosen by the *Sunday Times* (of London) "Hot 100" poll as one of three British architects most likely to impact their field in the next ten years. A member of the Royal Institute of British Architects (RIBA) since 1989, she sits on several professional committees and awards panels and is chair of the Jane Drew Prize, founded to celebrate diversity and inclusiveness in architectural activity.

Wigglesworth is also a professor of architecture at the University of Sheffield, an appointment she started in January 1999. Committed to improving the representation of women in architecture, she has lectured worldwide—most recently at the Architectural Association in London and the Canadian Centre for Architecture in Montreal—and has been extensively published.

Selected Awards

Honorable Mention, European competition for the Axelsberg site (in Stockholm, Sweden), 1993. Project exhibited at RIBA Headquarters in April 1994 and at City Hall, Stockholm in May 1994.

Fulbright Fellowship in Architecture, 1990–1991

Best Exhibit Award, Royal Academy of Arts Summer Exhibition, *Architects' Journal* and Bovis, 1986

Selected Publications

Baird, Iona, ed. *100 Architects from Across the World*. London: Phaidon Press, 2000.

Buxton, Pamela. "Profile on Sarah Wigglesworth and Jeremy Till." Blueprint, January 1999: 10–11.

Pearman, Hugh. *Contemporary World Architecture*. London: Phaidon Press, 1998, p. 212.

Slavid, Ruth. "People." *Architects' Journal*, 5 November 1998: 28–29.

Wigglesworth, Sarah. "My Life—in Theory," *Building Design*, 6 February 1998: 35.

FIRM PROFILE

Founded in 1993, Sarah Wigglesworth Architects seeks to diversify the conventional practice of architecture and to explore innovative forms of procurement, collaboration, and technology. While interested principally in building construction, the firm believes that this activity relies on the input of cross-disciplinary activities. To this end, it embraces the contributions of other branches of architectural research as well as of related disciplines. The practice has access to research facilities in academia, investigates grants and fundraising opportunities where appropriate, and has acted as manager and contractor on projects as demanded.

The firm's range of work includes sports and arts facilities, offices, bio-climatic housing, and exhibition design. Committed to using readily available and economical materials in an inventive way, Sarah Wigglesworth Architects produces designs that are accessible, fun, and provocative. The practice targets projects that allow thoughtful, critical dialogue with clients and that permit a challenging theoretical, spatial, or material exploration to take place. It aims to create sustainable architecture wherever possible, and to bring the debate concerning green buildings to the architectural mainstream.

Selected Clients

Bullitt Ltd.
Field Day Theatre Company
Packaging Innovation Ltd.
The Siobhan Davies Dance Company
Tonic Design
University College, London

DESIGN STATEMENT

Our most challenging project to date was the Straw House and Office in North London.

This project, designed in association with Jeremy Till, was for a house and associated studio office on an abandoned industrial site in North London. In it, we, the architects, have acted as developers and also intend to occupy the finished buildings. We identified the site; acquired it at auction; raised the finances; designed the buildings; negotiated with planning and building authorities, the railways, and neighbors; and researched

new technologies. We developed new construction methods and a new aesthetic for environmentally friendly buildings. The project is intended to demonstrate the potential for innovation in sustainable living in an urban environment.

The orientation of the buildings is used to optimize environmental conditions on the site. The northernmost elevation is wrapped with a heavily insulated straw-bale wall, while the southern elevation is glazed to capture solar heat and admit light. A five-story tower of books rises through the roof, providing a lookout reading room at the top. In the summer, the tower acts as a thermal flue, encouraging natural ventilation to cool the house. The roof is made of earth and is planted with a wildflower meadow.

Materials have been chosen with a view to limiting their environmental impact. Straw is cheap, recyclable, and an effective insulator. It has very low embodied energy (the energy used in its production) and is simple to use. Each bale is clad in galvanized steel sheeting, a prototype system that was developed by the architects with a view to wider usage, particularly in the housing sector.

The project also includes a large studio office, one wall of which faces a railway line. This wall is faced in sandbags for acoustic protection; the remaining walls are upholstered in a padded "bandage" of waterproof cloth, like a duvet. The office also incorporates the first-ever domestic use of gabion walls (the steel cages often seen retaining banks of earth), which are used as a series of piers to support the office floors above. They are filled with recycled concrete from other construction sites, thus avoiding landfill. Rainwater from the roof is collected in tanks and is pumped up to irrigate the meadow on the roof, fill closet cisterns in the office (which hold water for flushing the toilets), and feed the domestic washing machine.

ILLUSTRATED PROJECTS

Straw House and Office, North London, UK, designed 1996, completion of construction 2000

The Blue Land, Plymouth, UK, 1998

Writer's Cabin, North London, UK, 1999

Strawbale House & Office/Stock Orchard Street, North London, UK: 1 View of model from above, showing the rooftop wildflower meadow and lookout reading room; 2 View of model from railway; 3 View of model from the north, showing the straw bale wall; 4 Steel frame of the office with insertion of mezzanine; 5 Plan of first floor showing the house (top) and office (right); 6&7 Steel wall construction. Photo credit: Paul Smoothy [1–3]; courtesy Sarah Wigglesworth Architects [4, 6, 7]

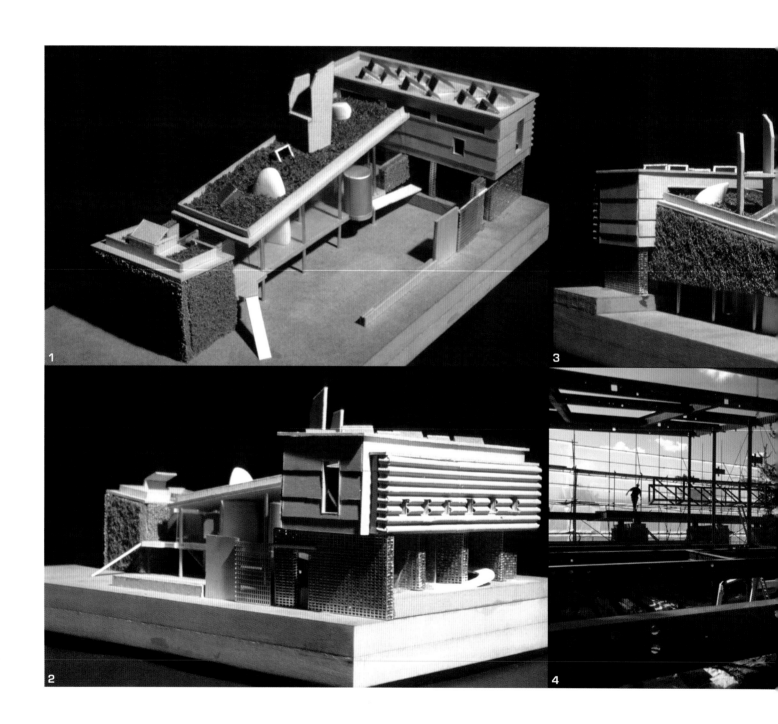

5

6

7

Writer's Cabin, North London, UK: 1 Sketch of interior; 2&3 Views from the garden. The design allows for multiple views of the surrounding woods, with light penetrating from all directions; 4 Interior view, showing daybed perched in rear wall. The cabin offers a variety of places for sitting, thinking, writing, and reading; 5 Interior view, showing writer's desk. All of the materials used were cheap, readily available, and chosen with a view to sustainability. Photo credit: Paul Smoothy

The Blue Land, Plymouth, UK: 1 South elevation, designed to take advantage of solar gain to reduce the heating load in winter; 2 East to west section, 3 North elevation. North walls are earth-sheltered and heavily insulated; 4 Axonometric from southwest; 5 View from east, showing all six houses on the site, designed to exploit the site's natural contours; 6 East to west site section. Photo credit: Sarah Wigglesworth Architects

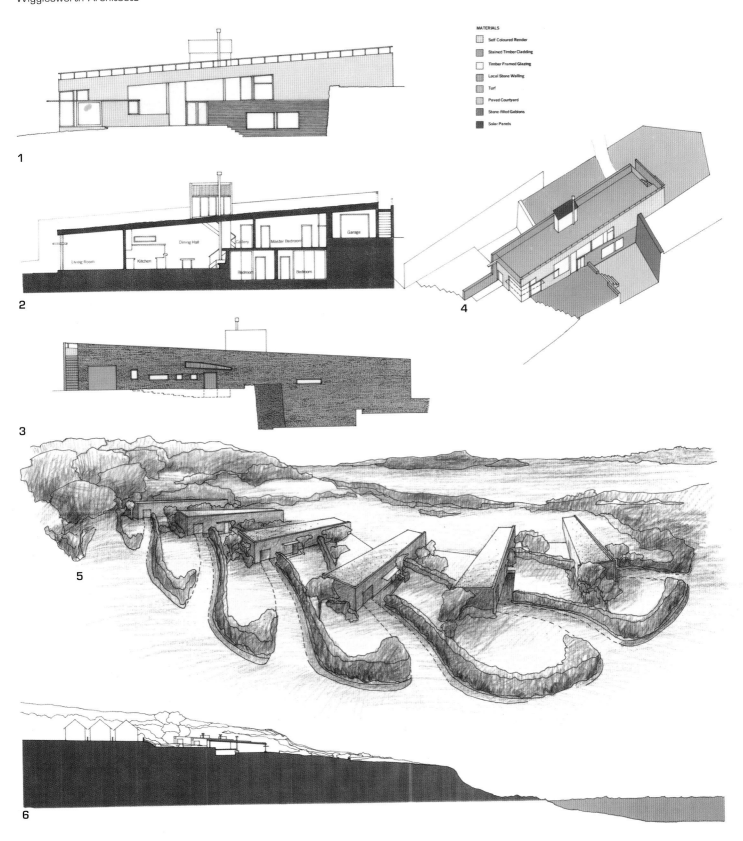

Contact Details

Irena Bauman
Bauman Lyons Architects Ltd.
Regent House
15 Hawthorn Road
Leeds LS7 4PH
UK
Tel: 011 44 113 294 4200
Fax: 011 44 113 294 1234
Email: irena@baumanlyons.co.uk

Ann Beha
Ann Beha Associates, Inc.
33 Kingston Street
Boston, Massachusetts 02111
Tel: 1 617 338 3000
Fax: 1 617 482 9097
Email: ABeha@ANNBEHA.com

Caroline Bos
UN Studio/Van Berkel & Bos BV
Stadhouderskade 113
1073 AX Amsterdam
The Netherlands
Tel: 011 31 20 570 2040
Fax: 011 31 20 570 2041
Email: info@unstudio.com

Alison Brooks
Alison Brooks Architects
35 Britannia Row
London N1 8QH
UK
Tel: 011 44 207 704 8808
Fax: 011 44 207 704 8409
Email: alison@ABAspace.com

Lise Anne Couture
Asymptote Architecture
561 Broadway, Suite 5A
New York, New York 10012
Tel: 1 212 343 7333
Fax: 1 212 343 7099
Email: info@asymptote.net

Odile Decq
Odile Decq Benoît Cornette
11, rue des Arquebusiers
Paris 75003
France
Tel: 011 33 1 4271 2741
Fax: 011 33 1 4271 2742

Elizabeth Diller
Diller + Scofidio
36 Cooper Square
New York, New York 10003
Tel: 1 212 260 7971
Fax: 1 212 260 7924
Email: disco2@flashcom.net

Julie Eizenberg
Koning Eizenberg Architecture
1454 25th Street
Santa Monica, California 90404
Tel: 1 310 828 6131
Fax: 1 310 828 0719
Email: info@kearch.com

Merrill Elam
Mack Scogin Merrill Elam Architects
75 John Wesley Dobbs Avenue
Atlanta, Georgia 30303
Tel: 1 404 525 6869
Fax: 1 414 525 7061
Email: office@msmearch.com

Karen Fairbanks
Marble • Fairbanks Architects
66 West Broadway, Suite 600
New York, New York 10007
Tel: 1 212 233 0653
Fax: 1 212 233 0654
Email: info@marble.fairbanks.com

Zaha Hadid
The Office of Zaha Hadid
Studio 9, 10 Bowling Green Lane
London EC1R 0BQ
UK
Tel: 011 44 207 253 5147
Fax: 011 44 207 251 8322
Email: zaha@hadid.u-net.com

Frances Halsband
R.M. Kliment & Frances Halsband
   Architects
255 West 26th Street
New York, New York 10001
Tel: 1 212 234 7400
Fax: 1 212 633 9769
Email: info@kliment-halsband.com

Gisue Hariri & Mojgan Hariri
Hariri & Hariri
18 East 12th Street
New York, New York 10003
Tel: 1 212 727 0338
Fax: 1 212 727 0479
Email: gh@haririandhariri.com

Jane Harrison
atopos
22 Constable House
Adelaide Road
London NW3 3QA
UK
Tel: 011 44 207 586 3446
Fax: 011 44 207 916 4287
Email: Atopos8@aol.com

Itsuko Hasegawa
Itsuko Hasegawa Atelier
1-9-7 Yushima, Bunkyo-ku
Tokyo 113-0034
Japan
Tel: 011 81 3 3818 5470
Fax: 011 81 3 3818 1821
Email: iha-sec@mx1.nisiq.net

Laurie Hawkinson
Smith-Miller + Hawkinson Architects
305 Canal Street
New York, New York 10013
Tel: 1 212 966 3875
Fax: 1 212 966 3877
Email: contact@smharch.com

Christine Hawley
Christine Hawley Architects
2nd Floor, 1–19 Torrington Place
London WC1E 6BT
UK
Tel: 011 44 207 504 5901
Fax: 011 44 207 380 7453
Email: chawley@ucl.ac.uk

Margaret Helfand
Helfand Myerberg Guggenheimer Architects
428 Broadway
New York, New York 10013
Tel: 1 212 925 2900
Fax: 1 212 925 9257
Email: hmga@hmga.com

Contact Details continued

Katharine Heron
Feary + Heron Architects
9 Huguenot Place
Heneage Street
London E1 5IJ
UK
Tel: 011 44 207 377 8663
Fax: 011 44 207 377 5199
Email: archfeary@compuserve.com

Lady Patty Hopkins
Michael Hopkins and Partners
27 Broadley Terrace
London NW1 6LG
UK
Tel: 011 44 207 724 1751
Fax: 011 44 207 723 0932
Email: hopkins@hopkins.co.uk

Cathi House
House + House
1499 Washington Street
San Francisco, California 94109
Tel: 1 415 474 2112
Fax: 1 415 474 2654
Email: house@ix.netcom.com

Eva Jiricna
Eva Jiricna Architects Limited
38 Warren Street, 3rd Floor
London W1P 5PD
UK
Tel: 011 44 207 554 2400
Fax: 011 44 207 388 8022
Email: mail@dircon.co.uk

Sulan Kolatan
Kolatan/MacDonald Studio
520 West 114 Street, Suite 41
New York, New York 10025-7809
Tel: 1 212 864 3051
Fax: 1 212 864 3051
Email: ask3@columbia.edu

Eve Laron
Eve Laron Architects
18 Monash Avenue
Killara, New South Wales 2071
Australia
Tel: 011 61 2 9498 4187
Fax: 011 61 2 9498 3543

M.J. Long
Long & Kentish Architects
Clarendon Buildings
27 Horsell Road
London N5 1XL
UK
Tel: 011 44 207 607 5658
Fax: 011 44 207 607 5621
Email: mail@longkentish.com

Victoria Meyers
Hanrahan + Meyers Architects
22 West 21st Street, 12th Floor
New York, New York 10010
Tel: 1 212 989 6026
Fax: 1 212 255 3776
Email: VLMHMA@aol.com

Carme Pinós
Carme Pinós Studio
Avda Diagonal 490
Barcelona 08006
Spain
Tel: 011 34 93 416 0372
Fax: 011 34 93 415 3719
Email: estpinos@arquired.es

Regina Pizzinini
Pizzinini/Luxemburg
2828 Donald Douglas Loop North, Suite 27
Santa Monica, California 90405
Tel: 1 310 452 9667
Fax: 1 310 452 9697
Email: pizzi@netway.at

Kazuyo Sejima
Kazuyo Sejima + Ryue Nishizawa
7-A, 2-2-35, Higashi-Shinagawa-Ku
Tokyo 140-0002
Japan
Tel: 011 81 3 3450 1754
Fax: 011 81 3 3450 1757
Email: sanaa@sanaa.co.jp

Laurinda Spear
Arquitectonica
550 Brickell Avenue, Suite 200
Miami, Florida 33131
Tel: 1 305 372 1812
Fax: 1 305 273 1175
Email: arq@arqintl.com

Billie Tsien
Tod Williams Billie Tsien and Associates
    Architects
222 Central Park South
New York, New York 10019
Tel: 1 212 582 2385
Fax: 1 212 245 1984
Email: mail@twbta.com

Nanako Umemoto
Reiser + Umemoto
200 West 92nd Street, Apt. 4B
New York, New York 10025
Tel: 1 212 421 8880
Fax: 1 212 496 7636
Email: rurarch@inch.com

Sarah Wigglesworth
Sarah Wigglesworth Architects
10 Stock Orchard Street
London N2 9RW
UK
Tel: 011 44 207 607 9200
Fax: 011 44 207 607 5800
Email: mail@swarch.co.uk

Acknowledgments

DATE DUE

NOV 2 6 2002

Watson-Guptill wishes to thank all participating firms for their valuable contribution to this publication.

Every effort has been made to trace the original source of copyright material contained in this book. The publishers would be pleased to hear from copyright holders to rectify any errors or omissions.

The information and illustrations in this publication have been prepared and supplied by the entrants. While all reasonable efforts have been made to source the required information and ensure accuracy, the publishers do not, under any circumstances, accept responsibility for errors, omissions, and representations express or implied.